T

FOCALG

tc

Camera

Accessories

THE (f) FOCALGUIDES TO

	Basic Photography
COLOUR	David Lynch
EFFECTS AND TRICKS	Günter Spitzing
EXPOSURE	David Lynch
LIGHTING	Paul Petzold
LOW LIGHT PHOTOGRAPHY	Paul Petzold
SLIDES	Graham Saxby
	Equipment
CAMERA ACCESSORIES	Leonard Gaunt
CAMERAS	Clyde Reynolds
FILTERS	Clyde Reynolds
FLASH	Günter Spitzing
LARGER FORMAT CAMERAS	Sidney Ray
LENSES	Leonard Gaunt
SLIDE-TAPE	Brian Duncalf
35 mm	Leonard Gaunt
THE 35 mm SINGLE-LENS REFLEX	Leonard Gaunt
	Processing
CIBACHROME	Jack H. Coote
COLOUR FILM PROCESSING	Derek Watkins
COLOUR PRINTING	Jack H. Coote
THE DARKROOM	Leonard Gaunt
ENLARGING	Günter Spitzing
HOME PROCESSING	Ralph Jacobson
	Subjects
ACTION PHOTOGRAPHY	Don Morley
CLOSE-UPS	Sidney Ray
MOUNTAINS	Douglas Milner
PHOTOGRAPHING PEOPLE	Alison Trapmore
PLANTS AND FLOWERS	David Walton
PORTRAITS	Günter Spitzing
	Movie
MOVIEMAKING	Paul Petzold
SHOOTING ANIMATION	Zoran Perisic

The FOCALGUIDE to Camera Accessories

Leonard Gaunt

Focal Press · London

Focal/Hastings House · New York

BL British Library Cataloguing in Publication Data

Gaunt, Leonard
The Focalguide to Camera Accessories
— (Focalguides).
1. Photography—Apparatus and supplies
I. Title II. Series
771.3 TR265

ISBN (excl. USA) 0 240 51043 7
ISBN (USA only) 0 8038 2385 1

Filmset and printed in Great Britain by
Thomson Litho Ltd, East Kilbride, Scotland.

Contents

Who Needs Accessories ?

When you buy a camera you may think you are fully equipped to take pictures, but the camera is only the beginning. There are accessories.

If you are a beginner and you are wise, you will have bought a relatively simple camera. That is the best choice because the number of additional items you can be persuaded to attach to it or use in conjunction with it, is limited. You are in the fortunate position of being able to learn how to use your camera without too many distractions.

For those who buy a more 'advanced' or sophisticated camera, escape is not so easy. Even if they buy it unseen in a box, they will soon be made aware either by friends or press advertisements or, eventually, by the instruction book, that they can fit wide-angle and long-focus lenses to it. They will learn that special close-up equipment is available and will almost certainly feel that a selection of filters is indispensable.

Then there is flash. It could cost nearly as much as the camera—and there are accessories for flashguns, too.

A tripod may not immediately spring to mind (although it soon will) but what about an easily portable camera clamp, baby tripod, pistol grip, or rifle grip for the long lens?

Can you really call yourself a photographer without a separate exposure meter, even though your camera is fully automated? Perhaps you should give a passing thought to a gadget for copying your slides and surely a look-around-the-corner angle finder is not a luxury?

If you travel you must have a case, holdall or bag in which to carry all your equipment. If you go abroad, you also want a special bag to protect your films from airport security X-rays.

There is an almost limitless supply of extras for all occasions. Do you really need all or any of them?

All-in-one cameras

There are a lot of very simple cameras that are designed to do the entire job. Most of the cartridge-loading cameras fall into this category. They make very good work of taking pictures in reasonable lighting conditions—which is all most camera users want. They are rarely designed to take any extra equipment beyond perhaps a flash unit and occasionally a filter and/or close-up lens. Slightly more advanced models may even have those extras built in and cannot usefully be fitted with anything else.

Advancing a little further and also moving into the field of cameras that use 35 mm or larger film, there are fixed-lens cameras for which a rather greater variety of accessories is available. Still not a vast amount, however, because the lens cannot be removed from these cameras, and quite a lot of accessories are designed to fit behind the lens.

The ultimate of course, is the interchangeable-lens camera. These are now nearly all single-lens-reflex cameras—the type that use the camera lens to project the image on to the viewfinder screen, instead of having a separate little optical system above the lens. There are still one or two interchangeable-lens 35 mm cameras that are not SLRs but, in general, the relatively low-priced 35 mm camera is a fixed-lens type. If you want a camera that can take a wide selection of different lenses, you have to have a moderately expensive SLR. The interchangeable-lens non-reflex camera can be fitted with only a limited range of alternative lenses.

It is the SLR and mainly the 35 mm SLR that attracts the major efforts of the accessory manufacturers.

System cameras

Interchangeable-lens cameras are often called system cameras because the ability to remove the lens and replace it by another optical system means that the camera can be used for almost any type of photography. It can be used in conjunction with extension tubes or bellows to allow the lens to focus closer than its built-in mechanism allows. It can even dispense with the lens and be fitted to a microscope to provide greatly magnified images. It can also be used on giant telescopes.

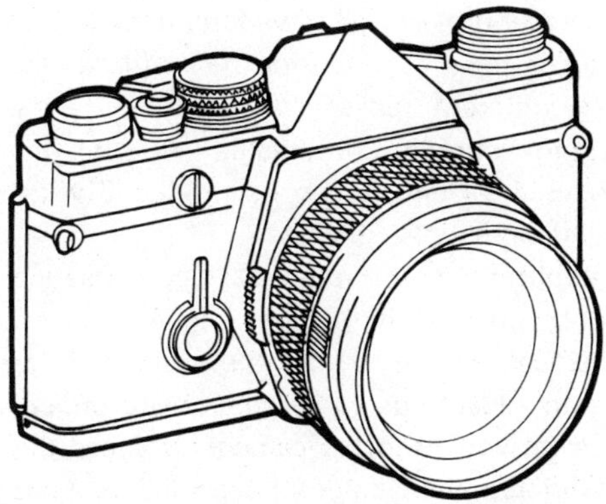

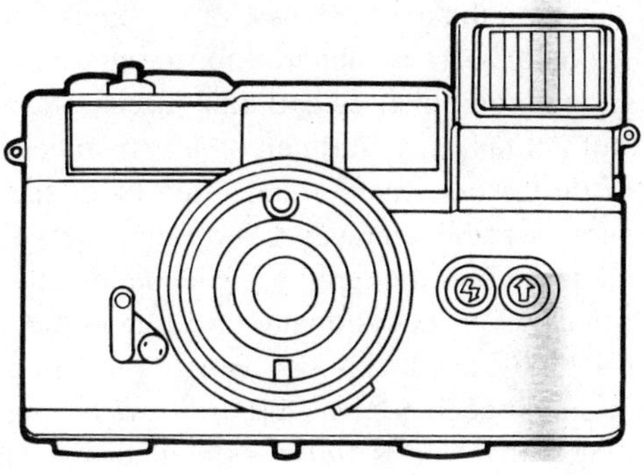

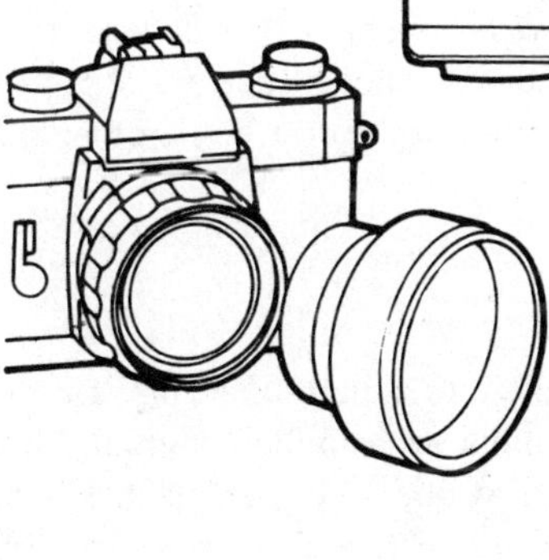

The single-lens reflex is easily recognized by the characteristic hump formed by the pentaprism. These cameras invariably have interchangeable lenses. Most cameras with viewfinders independent of the lens have just one lens that cannot be changed. A few SLRs have lenses with a fixed rear component and interchangeable front components.

An almost infinite selection of lenses of various focal lengths and other characteristics can be substituted for the normal or standard lens. You can use different lenses for portraits, landscapes, architecture, long-range sporting or wildlife subjects, cramped interiors and so on. Special effects can be produced with ultra-wide-angle lenses and extreme telephotos.

For most of these applications, the reflex design is essential. The non-reflex just cannot cope with the focusing and viewfinding difficulties of too radical a change from the normal or standard lens. The reflex design allows you to see the image projected by whatever optical system you fit to the camera, whereas the non-reflex has to have a different viewfinder for each lens or a means of adjusting the angle of view of the built-in finder.

It could be said that the true system camera is that for which a wide range of lenses and other accessories is specifically designed. But virtually any SLR can be a system camera because accessories made for one camera can often be adapted to fit another. Many such adapters are available off the shelf; others can be specifically made. In fact the term 'system camera' has no real meaning, but it serves as an occasionally useful label for the type of camera that can be used for a variety of photographic tasks. Any interchangeable-lens SLR is a system camera. No camera from which the lens is not designed to be removed can be a system camera; although it may be one specialized unit in an otherwise integrated system.

The need for accessories

Are your accessories really necessary? This may sound flippant but it is a serious question. Manufacturers will produce anything they think the public can be persuaded to buy. If you think that is an overstatement, remember the camera with a built-in radio—first offered in the 1960s.

Over the years manufacturers have done such a good job on filters that many a beginner has bought a camera and immediately asked the salesman 'What filters do I need?' Filters probably provide the outstanding example of unnecessary accessories. Of course, they have very real uses and no photographer concerned with the truest possible rendering of colours in garments, threads, textiles, etc. would be without his personal collection. But filters are sold in unbelievable quantities every year and it is a safe bet that a very large proportion of them are rarely, if ever, used.

Let us go to the other extreme and think of an accessory that is rarely used but should, in fact, be used much more. There are one or two candidates: lens hood (more for protection than its intended use) and, for the same reason, lens cap; tripod and its associated cable certainly. Beyond that it is very difficult to think of anything—except the shutter release finger, the most useful accessory of all. A lot of the time spent in amassing accessories could more usefully be spent in taking pictures.

Perhaps that is too cynical a viewpoint. Many accessories have a definite use and are invaluable for their particular purpose. If your photography involves a lot of extreme close-ups a set of extension tubes, or even a bellows unit is essential. Conversely, if you habitually find it necessary to shoot at relatively long range, you must have a lens of longer than normal focal length. In either case, and certainly in the first, you need a tripod and, preferably, a cable release. If you have a tripod, then you really should have a quick-release shoe—and so on.

How to choose accessories

When you buy an interchangeable-lens camera, you virtually commit yourself to buying accessories for it. There is nothing wrong with this, provided you first encounter the need for the accessory and then go looking for it, rather than vice-versa.

The need generally arises only when you habitually take pictures that call for a particular accessory. If you only occasionally take a close-up photograph it might make more sense to buy an inexpensive supplementary lens and improvise a camera stand, rather than invest what could be a really large sum of money in bellows, focusing slide, tripod, copy stand, macro lens, etc. For the occasional long shot, a tele-extender might make more sense than a telephoto lens or, with care, you can even manage with selective enlargement of part of the negative. A power winder makes little sense for everyday photography but is very useful for remote control work.

A clear pattern emerges. For everyday photography, in the fields, perhaps, of portraiture (even glamour) landscapes and scenics in general, shots of friends and relatives, their children and pets, general human activities at work and play and the hundred and one other subjects that make up most of the photographs taken every day, accessories are rarely necessary. Sometimes, admittedly, you might prefer a lens of other than the standard focal length. You are unlikely to need much more. For the specialist, exactly the opposite may apply. He often needs a particular accessory or range of accessories to enable him to do his job efficiently.

The system camera is designed to cater for specialist needs as well as everyday photography. The specialist item may be no more than a single extension tube. Or it might be a whole range of sophisticated equipment allowing the camera to focus, zoom, pan, tilt, assess its own exposure and take the picture from an almost endlessly remote location. Between these limits there are items for nearly every eventuality, and some that seek to create a use where none may have previously existed.

So once you have established a need for an accessory how do you go about buying it? The camera manufacturer will tell you that only his own products are suitable for his camera. That is rarely true and many camera manufacturers, particularly those using the popular 42 mm screw thread, actually rely on independent manufacturers to produce accessories that they themselves do not supply. The same independent manufacturers supply camera manufacturers with accessories that are then sold under the camera name.

You do have to be careful with some items. Despite attempts at standardization, there are still a lot of different methods of attaching lenses to cameras. Items that attach to the camera lens mount, therefore, tend to be unique to a particular camera. Independent manufacturers offer suitable products and they are often as efficient as the genuine article. Sometimes, however, they do not couple with all the automatic workings of that particular camera. If your camera has complicated electronic gadgetry, it might be as well to make careful enquiries before buying a lens-mount-attaching accessory of another make.

This applies specifically to lenses, of course. It is rarely an insuperable problem with such items as bellows and extension tubes. Despite the many so-called automatic bellows units available, few use anything more automatic than a double cable release or similar external coupling. Even fewer maintain full-aperture metering or any of the other sophisticated functions of some camera-attached lenses. In the circumstances in which bellows and tubes are used, such refinements are rarely of any particular value. The independent manufacturer's product, often a great deal less expensive, is generally perfectly satisfactory.

That is not however, a recommendation to buy the cheapest item available. In most cases, you get what you pay for and some accessories are very easy to make—badly. Lenses, bellows, tripods, filters and slide copiers are among the products that are available in relatively inexpensive versions. But by saving money you could easily be wasting it. A tripod with spindly legs or locks that need to be fastened with a wrench is likely to give worse results than if you supported the camera on a pile of books. If you cannot examine the product before you buy it, stick to the well-known names and be prepared to pay more than at the lower end of the market. If you have a real need for the product it must do its job well. If it does, the extra money is well spent.

Choose your accessories with as much care as you put in to choosing your camera. Most people recognize that there are vital differences between one camera and another: vital to them, that is, whether because they have small or large hands, or poor eyesight or because they have a particular need or preference. The same applies to many accessories. It is how they measure up in use that counts.

Looking at Lenses

There are specialist books on lenses, including the *Focalguide to Lenses* in this series, so we are here concerned only with the broader aspects. Alternative lenses are of interest only to the owner of an interchangeable-lens camera, i.e. a camera from which the lens can be simply twisted and unscrewed from the body or which has a more complicated but more easily operated bayonet-type attachment. Nearly all such cameras are single-lens reflex models, mostly 35 mm, with the characteristic pentaprism hump on the top. Very few non-reflex cameras and even fewer cartridge-loading types take interchangeable lenses.

Lenses for non-reflex cameras

A few manufacturers offer wide-angle and/or telephoto attachments for fixed camera lenses. These are designed to fit in front of the camera's standard lens, generally by screwing into the filter thread. They provide such a limited change of focal length that their use is pointless for black-and-white photography. Extra enlargement of the negative will almost certainly provide better quality. There may be an argument in favour of them for colour slide work but even there the value is doubtful, particularly as they can be quite expensive.

The loss in quality that inevitably results from the use of such attachments may be acceptable to some in the case of the so-called 'fish-eye' types. These provide a very wide angle of view totally unsuited to normal photography but occasionally useful as a special effect.

These remarks do not necessarily apply to the telephoto facility built into some cartridge-loading cameras. The small image provided by these cameras does not lend itself so easily to extra enlergement and, in any case, the facility is built in and not offered as an extra.

Finally, there have been various cameras over the years that used special two-part lenses—an interchangeable front component and a fixed rear component. The rear component, often incorporating a shutter, is permanently attached to the camera body. The front component can be removed and exchanged for another providing conversion to moderate wide-angle or telephoto capability. The interchangeable components are always unique to the particular camera but not often to the particular lens. Independent lens manufacturers do not produce alternative types for these cameras.

None of these attachments is a true interchangeable lens and, with the exception of the last-mentioned, the image quality they provide is, at best, barely acceptable. At worst, it has been lamentable.

Interchangeable lenses

The true interchangeable lens is a complete lens designed to be easily fitted to and removed from the camera body. The user is thus enabled to change the lens on his camera to suit a variety of different subjects.

The main characteristic of any photographic lens is the size of the image it produces. This is directly related to the focal length of the lens, which is the distance between the lens and a sharply focused image of a distant subject. When a sharp image of such a subject is formed 50 mm behind the lens, the focal length of that lens is 50 mm. You cannot easily measure that distance, because the measuring point is the optical centre of the lens and, in a complex lens, that could even be outside the physical limits of the lens. The question rarely arises, however, because the focal length is nearly always indicated on the lens.

The real significance of the focal length is that it indicates the relative image size which is, in general, proportional to focal length. A 200 mm lens gives an image four times larger than that from a 50 mm lens—an image, that is, of a particular object at a particular distance, not the total picture size. On a given film size, therefore, the lens with the longer focal length takes in less of the view before it, i.e. it has a narrower angle of view. The effect is similar to that of the view through a telescope compared with what the unaided eye sees.

There are three main groups of camera lens—wide-angle, normal or standard, and long-focus or telephoto.

Standard lenses

The standard lens generally fitted to a camera when you buy it has an angle of view of about 46°. On a 35 mm camera that means a focal length of 50 mm or thereabouts. There are exceptions, but that is the most popular angle for a standard lens.

The 46° angle of view is chosen as that which gives roughly the same perspective impression of the subject as the human eye. In other words, objects at various distances from the camera are reproduced in about the relative sizes you would expect. It is an approximation, of course, and relies on your viewing the whole image area and not just part of it.

The angle of view is not a prime function of the lens itself. It depends on the size of the film. A 50 mm lens has about a 46° angle of view on 35 mm film but a wider angle (about 80°) on 6×6 cm film. Lenses are generally made for particular cameras, however, and a 50 mm lens for a 35 mm camera would not normally provide very good image quality outside the central 36 mm-diameter circle.

Wide-angle lens

As its description implies, the wide-angle lens covers a wider angle of view than the standard lens—commonly from about 60° to 90°, but even wider angles up to 180° are available as specialist lenses.

The wider angle naturally produces a smaller image of a given object but includes more of the scene around it. The perspective effect depends largely on the nature of the foreground. With recognizable objects close to the camera (the wide-angle lens can often focus closer than a standard lens) the perspective is steep. The nearby object looks a great deal larger than similar-size or even larger objects only a short distance away. Without recognizable objects close to the camera, the steep perspective is not so obvious

but very distant objects such as hills or mountains may be almost flattened by the small-scale reproduction.
Wide-angle lenses are not easy to make and good ones tend to be expensive. The wider the angle, the more difficult it is to prevent distortion creeping in—notably barrel distortion which causes straight lines away from the centre of the image to bow outward. Illumination may become uneven, too, causing some darkening of the corners of the picture.

Long-focus lenses

Long-focus lenses are those of longer focal length and thus narrower angle than the standard lens—from about 28° down to 2.5° or less on 35 mm cameras. Larger-format cameras tend to stop short of the extremes that are common with 35 mm models. Wide angles may stop at about 55° and long focus at approximately 5°.
Telephoto lenses are long-focus lenses of special construction that allows them to be made of shorter physical length than focal length. In all other aspects the two types are effectively the same and it is now common practice to call all long-focus lenses telephotos.
The narrow angle of the telephoto lens produces a larger image of a given object but includes less of the scene on the film. Where a 50 mm lens, for example, might give you an image about 5 mm high of a distant building, a 300 mm lens could increase that to 30 mm but would include much less of the surroundings. If you wanted the general scene to show the building and its milieu you might use a 50 mm lens. If the building alone was the main interest the 300 mm would be more appropriate.
The telephoto lens gives a characteristically flat perspective. As it is commonly used to shoot distant objects there is nothing nearby to establish the scene. There is no indication that *all* the objects in the picture are distant, so they look strangely similar in size despite their various distances from the camera. In a shot from the back of a hall the head of a speaker on the platform can look the same size as those of people sitting some distance behind him.
Perspective is not a function of the lens of course. It depends entirely on viewpoint. But the wide-angle lens is commonly used

at close range and the telephoto at long range, so there is no need to be too pedantic in a book of this nature. With a wide-angle lens, you commonly get steep perspective, with distances between objects looking greater than they actually are. With long-focus lenses, the opposite is generally apparent. Objects look closer together than they are.

Special constructions

Apart from the special telephoto construction, there are various other types of lens that have been designed to do something different. The zoom is probably the best known.

A zoom lens has an extra control that rearranges the internal components of the lens to change its focal length within prescribed limits. A 40–80 mm zoom, for example, can be used as a lens of any focal length from 40 mm to 80 mm, thus varying the scale of reproduction (image size:object size) over the range 1:2. It is, in effect, a moderate wide angle, a standard lens and a moderate telephoto (on a 35 mm camera) all in one.

You don't get all that for nothing. Whereas a normal 40 mm lens would probably focus down to about 30 cm or less and have a maximum aperture of *f*2.8 or greater, your zoom might focus no closer than 2 m and have a maximum aperture of *f*3.5. In a short zoom such as this, however, there could be an extra control to allow you to switch to a close-focusing (macro) range. We shall come to that in the close-up chapter.

A longer zoom, say 85–200 mm, would have the same close-focusing and maximum aperture limitations plus significant bulk, while the really big zooms (50–250 mm and similar) can be particularly cumbersome if you find yourself using the 'short end' and more often than not you probably would.

Another special construction is the mirror lens. Using reflecting surfaces (mirrors) in conjunction with ordinary lens components, the mirror lens shortens the light path between lens and film by effectively folding it up. The lens itself can therefore be made remarkably short for its focal length but, because the mirrors need space to reflect, it becomes much fatter. The mirror lens (generally available in focal lengths of 500 mm upwards) is used in exactly

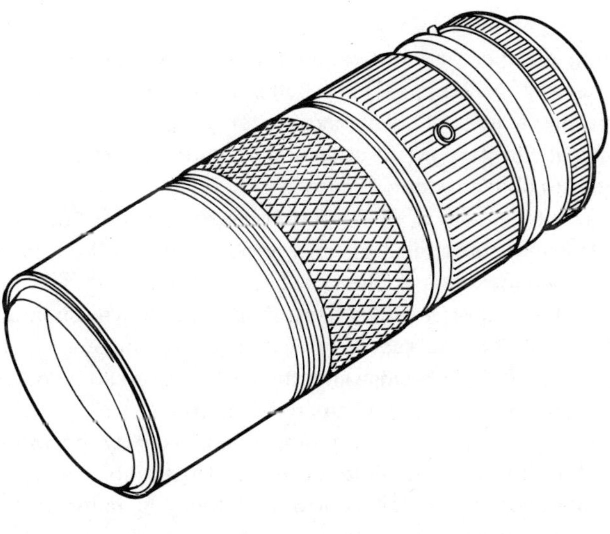

A zoom lens differs from others in that it has an extra control to vary focal length as well as distance and aperture. In some cases that means an extra control ring as in the lens above. In others, the zoom control is combined with the focusing ring in a push-pull operation.

the same manner as an orthodox lens except that it has no diaphragm. Light transmission has to be controlled by neutral-density or other filters. They have no diaphragm because there is a mirror in the centre of the lens at the front. This can introduce a characteristic 'hole-in-the-middle' or doughnut effect in out-of-focus highlights, demonstrating to your friends that you are the proud possessor of one of these instruments. It is strange how many mirror lens shots incorporate such highlights.

Lenses that can be tilted and shifted relative to film plane are another special construction. They give a certain amount of correction of converging lines caused by tilting the camera and also extend your control over depth of field.

Among the other 'specials' is a variable-field-curvature type in which the plane of sharp focus can be 'bent' into a curve to provide unusual depth of field (or lack of it) effects.

Choosing lenses

The choice of an additional lens often comes down to a matter of shooting distance. If you like getting close to your subject (and you often get greater impact and better quality that way), you need a wide-angle lens. If, like many other people, you are a little hesitant at the thought of approaching your subject too closely, you tend to choose a long-focus lens.

That is not actually a very good basis for choice. The subject should govern the choice of lens. Shooting from a long way off with a telephoto lens is not a substitute for shooting at closer range with a shorter focus lens. The perspective often looks 'wrong' and the subject can get lost in unnaturally large background detail. In a close shot the background can be dwarfed, and sometimes even hidden behind the subject.

On the other hand, the wide-angle lens is only occasionally satisfactory for wide-ranging views of large subjects such as landscapes. Distant detail is lost and there is rather a lot of foreground and sky.

Wide-angle lenses are particularly suitable for many interior shots, shooting in crowds or narrow streets, close-ups of particular features plus a reasonable amount of background detail, and, of course, special subjects with deliberately distorted perspective.

Telephoto lenses are virtually essential for subjects you simply cannot approach closely—such as many sporting events, processions, timid or ferocious animals, ground-to-air shots, etc. Even portraits can benefit from the slightly more pleasant modelling provided by the moderate telephoto.

You have to be careful about going to extremes. Very wide-angle lenses have limited uses. As they can be expensive think hard before buying. Very long-focus lenses can be difficult to handle. Even though some are now remarkably compact, they need only the tiniest movement in your hands to cause the large image on the film to move appreciably and give you a blurred picture. Image quality can also suffer simply because of the great distance between camera and subject. Heat haze, mist and other atmospheric conditions may reduce both contrast and detail.

Zoom lenses enable you to frame your subjects exactly as you wish, without having to rely on subsequent masking for projection or selective enlargement in printing. That can be useful if you have the eye of a Cartier-Bresson and a precise knowledge of the extent of viewfinder and slide mount omissions. There is the advantage of being able to vary the focal length, and thus image size, at will. But look at the specification carefully and see what you are losing. Take special note of maximum aperture and bulk. There is little sense in loading yourself down with a rather slow, weighty lens when you do a lot of work in poor light and one focal length predominates.

The choice of lenses must be geared to the type of work you do most often. An expensive long-focus, wide-angle or zoom lens can be a real burden if you badly overestimate the applications you have for it.

Using lenses

A point that seems to worry many people unfamiliar with changing lenses is the idea that different focal lengths call for different handling. In fact, virtually every photographic lens works in exactly the same way. For example, when you put a telephoto lens on a reflex camera it projects an image on to the focusing screen in precisely the same way as any other lens—and that is the image that will appear on the film.

A telephoto lens does not call for extra exposure. The fact that when you enlarge the image on the film, you have to let extra light through the lens to allow for the dimmer image, often seems to be misunderstood. It *is* a fact, but the lens takes care of it automatically by the *f*-number system. When you set *f*4 on a 100 mm lens you are actually setting a larger physical aperture than you do at *f*4 on a 50 mm lens. That allows for the extra distance the light has to travel inside the lens and the spread of the image to ensure that the light level at the film is the same in both cases. A given *f*-number lets the same amount of light reach the film whatever the focal length of the lens.

Of course, there can be differences in the pictorial effects created by different lenses and you have to handle long or heavy lenses with some care to avoid camera shake, but the mechanical aspects are the same with any lens. The use of close-up equipment for example, is not confined to standard lenses. Supplementary lenses, extension tubes and bellows (see the chapter on close-ups) can be used just as effectively with any lens. A short extension tube on a long-focus lens is often quite useful for photographing small objects from a reasonable shooting distance.

There is no need to fear that the purchase of another lens requires you to adjust your handling methods or make tiresome calculations. You just get a larger or smaller image, nothing else. What you make of that facility is up to you or down to you, depending on your idiom.

What You Can Do with Filters

The number of different lenses that you can attach to your camera can cause some confusion. As they are rather expensive, however, lenses are not often bought on the spur of the moment. Economic considerations impose a certain amount of thought. On the other hand, there is an extraordinary range of lens attachments on the market and many of them are moderately inexpensive. It is easy to be persuaded that they are essential.

What are filters for?

If you want the complete answer to that question, read the *Focalguide to Filters,* which points out the genuine uses of filters for those who have a real need for them. Here, we are confined to basics and to showing that the possession of a fine collection of filters should not become an obsession.

Most camera filters are coloured—dyed in the mass glass. Some expensive types consist of gelatin in a glass sandwich. The colour of the filter modifies the colour of the light reflected from the various parts of the subject before it passes through the camera lens to the film. With a yellow filter, for example, the effect is rather as if you were looking at the subject through a sheet of yellow glass, or as if you had put a yellow wash over a colour painting of your subject.

In a colour picture the yellows, reds and mixtures thereof, might not be very affected, but the blues, some green and other colours containing blue, are darkened and rendered very impure. That is not a desirable effect with most colour pictures but it has its uses in black and white.

Black-and-white film is panchromatic, i.e. it reacts to light of all colours. It does not reproduce the colours but it darkens according to the brilliance of the light. So a yellow filter, by its different effect on different colours, changes the relative brilliances and hence the tonal rendering of the subject. A brilliantly blue sky reproduces darker through a yellow filter than if the filter had not been used, while no noticeable change takes place in other parts of the subject not containing blue.

All coloured filters work on the principle of selectively absorbing light of certain colours. The effect is most pronounced with colours furthest apart in the spectrum. As the spectrum of white light runs through red, orange, yellow, green, blue and violet, it is readily seen that yellow has some effect on blue, while red and orange have a greater effect, and vice-versa.

Filters for black-and-white

So the main function of coloured filters for black-and-white photography is to alter the effect on the film of coloured subjects, thus 'falsifying' the tonal rendering. That can be necessary for various reasons but more often than not in order to separate subjects or parts of a subject that are similar in brilliance but different in colour.

White clouds in a blue sky are a common example. Black-and-white films are a little over-sensitive to blue, seeing it as rather lighter than the eye sees it. Thus, clouds that are clearly visible to the eye sometimes appear much less well defined in a black-and-white photograph. Put on a yellow filter and the blue is held back somewhat and rendered darker in the final image. You can go further and exaggerate the effect by using a deeper yellow or orange or red filter.

Nevertheless, a filter is not necessary every time clouds and a blue sky appear in your picture. Modern films are quite capable of rendering cloudscapes satisfactorily without a filter. If you do not find that so, the probability is that you are overexposing, allowing the blue sky so much exposure that it 'catches up' with the white cloud.

In any case, you should not use a filter for such scenes without first studying the rest of the subject carefully. Blue clothing, flowers, paintwork, etc. will also be darkened, while yellow, orange and some red objects may be rendered in too light a tone. If you use an orange or red filter for a really dramatic sky, some brickwork may go virtually white.

Therefore restrain your enthusiasm for filters and use them only when absolutely necessary. Flowers can sometimes benefit from the filter treatment when the tonal brilliance of the bloom is almost the same as that of the surrounding foliage. Lettering on coloured backgrounds may stand out well to the eye but need filtration to render it satisfactorily in black and white. Specialist tasks like photographing postmarks across coloured stamps or envelopes, faded and/or discoloured documents, tissue sections in microscopy, etc. often demand carefully controlled filtration to increase contrast, but day-to-day photography rarely needs it.

Filters, however good their quality, are just flat pieces of material. Used in front of the lens, as they normally are, they must affect image quality. The degradation may be minimal but it can take the edge off the performance of the lens. There is no point in that unless the filter is being used for a real purpose.

Filters for colour photography

There is even less reason to use filters in colour photography than in black-and-white unless you are after special effects. Their function is the same but in this case they affect the colour, as well as the brilliance, of the various tones of the subject. Consequently, filters for colour photography are very much paler in colour. The relatively strong filters used for black-and-white are usable only for effect. The weakest yellow filter, for example, would put a noticeable yellow tinge or cast over the whole scene.

Colour film, however, is sensitive to the actual colour characteristics of the light used for photography. It needs what is generally called white light which approximates to daylight in the middle hours of a sunny day with some cloud in the sky. In early morning and late afternoon, or when the sky is heavily overcast or exceptionally clear, the colour of daylight departs from the ideal and the colours in your picture can be distorted.

Often that is no disadvantage. If you are shooting a sunset you generally want it to look like a sunset, with a preponderance of yellow or red in the scene. You would expect some neutral, and even flesh tones, to be tinged with the sunset effect. In dull conditions you may well wish the picture to show the dullness. At other times you may want to use a filter to offset these conditions. A bluish filter compensates for the yellow effect of sunset (or sunrise sometimes) and is often called a 'morning and evening' filter. It does not produce a morning or evening effect; it kills it. You use it on the rare occasions when you are shooting at these times of the day and wish to make it look as if you were shooting at midday. Similarly, you can use an amber or straw-coloured filter to warm up the tones of a scene in dull weather or in an excess of blue light.

The 'warming up' filter can, in fact, have many genuine uses. The palest is often called a 'skylight' filter and that gives a clue to its most valid use. Strong sunlight in a cloudless sky can cause too powerful contrasts for some colour pictures, notably outdoor portraits. In such conditions you could take your subject into the shadow of a building. That gives lower contrast but by cutting out the direct sunlight it leaves all the light to come from a blue sky. You may not notice it, but the film does, and your picture has a distinct cool-colour effect. A skylight filter can make a noticeable improvement. Some photographers regularly use a slightly stronger salmon filter on dull days to relieve the rather strong blue-green that sometimes appears in these conditions.

Ultraviolet filters

Some colour workers make much ado about the use of a UV filter—ultra-violet absorbing. Ultra-violet is a 'colour' beyond the visible end of the spectrum. It cannot be seen but both black-and-white and colour film are sensitive to it. It is most noticeable in colour as it causes a blue colour cast similar to that from sunless skylighting.

Ultra-violet radiation (we should not call it light, because it is invisible) is generally present only in very clear air. Being a very shortwave radiation it is easily absorbed by the tiny solid particles in the normal atmosphere and, as all lenses absorb a certain amount of ultra-violet, very little gets through to the film. In sunlight after heavy rainfall, high up in mountain areas or near large stretches of water, however, the air is cleaner and ultra-violet radiation can be troublesome.

Again, don't rush to the filter. A bluish tinge to mountain scenery is not at all unexpected. When it is too strong a UV filter can be helpful but you may well find that your camera lens absorbs quite enough of the UV to make a satisfying, only slightly blue picture. If you use a skylight or darker salmon filter that also absorbs UV, you do not need a separate UV filter as well. Colourless, the UV filter has no effect on visible colours but it restrains the over-blue effect of the ultra-violet, sometimes effectively reducing blueness in complexions and other lighter colours in colour photography. It generally has little effect on the distant blue haze in landscapes, however. That is more likely to be caused by the scattering of visible blue light by the atmosphere and is more effectively treated by haze-cutting orange or red filters in black-and-white, or amber filters for colour.

Polarizing screens

The usefulness of a single polarizing filter or screen is somewhat overplayed. Polarizing material is made from a special type of material that acts like a slotted filter, transmitting only those light waves that vibrate in the direction of the slots. Light polarized in one plane can thus pass fully through the filter only when the slots are correctly oriented.

The theory is fine. Some light—notably that reflected from glass and some other shiny surfaces—is plane polarized, but only when the light falls on it (is incident upon it) at a certain angle. Shoot from that angle (the angle of incidence is equal to the angle of reflection) with a polarizing filter rotated so that the slots are at right angles to the plane of polarization and no reflections can get through. Ordinary (random) light from the scene passes relatively unhindered but the reflections are stopped.

Shoot from any angle other than this perfect angle and the polarizer has less and less effect until, when you reach the normal (at right angles to the reflecting surface) it has no effect at all. There, you can eliminate no reflection, which makes the polarizer hopeless for square-on photographs of shop windows, paintings under glass, etc. It is not even a lot of use to photograph oil paintings at the seemingly correct angle because reflections from the uneven surface come off at all angles.

Again, polarizing screens have legitimate uses, but mainly in pairs. One polarizer can be used to polarize all light passing through it, and another to control the amount reaching the film. We come to that shortly. You can use large sheets of the material to polarize the light from one lamp and light only part of the subject with it, and so selectively control subject lighting. With more sophisticated equipment in photomicrography you can set up specialist treatments of stress and structural photography that can also be turned into interesting abstract patterns—but that goes beyond the scope of this book.

A marginally justifiable use for the polarizing screen is that involving landscape or other photography that includes significant areas of blue sky. On a cloudless day you may often notice that part of the sky looks a much deeper blue than the rest. When you photograph into that blue colour, however, it tends to come out far less dramatically than you expected. That is because films are more sensitive to blue than the human eye. The polarizing filter can help because that very blue skylight is to some extent polarized by reflection from tiny moisture droplets in the atmosphere. A suitably oriented polarizing screen can cut out some of that polarized light and thus restore the deep blue that you see.

The particular advantage with colour films is that there is no effect on any part of in the scene.

Polarizing screens, like UV filters, can be used with black-and-white or colour film. The effects are similar but tend to be more dramatic in colour.

Neutral density filters

Neutral density only means density without colour. So neutral density filters can be used with both black-and-white and colour films. Their function is simply to reduce the amount of light reaching the film.

This is the filter that perhaps has the greatest justification for its existence and yet is the least often used. It has various applications

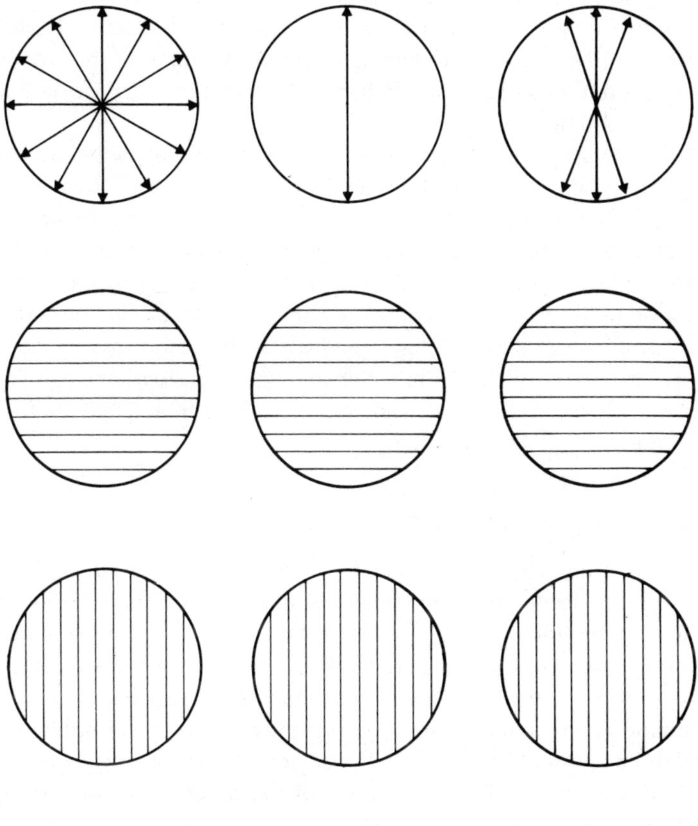

Random light (*top left*) radiates in all directions and passes almost unimpeded through a polarizing screen no matter how it is oriented. Perfectly plane-polarized light (*middle*) cannot pass through the screen oriented as immediately below but passes freely when the screen is rotated through 90 degrees. The more practical strongly polarized light (*right*) is strongly impeded by the polarizer in the first position but passes relatively freely when the screen is rotated through 90 degrees.

that are mostly related to its function as a substitute aperture control. You may remember that a mirror lens generally has no iris diaphragm because the central part of the lens is used for reflection. You cannot control light transmission by the normal aperture control so you use neutral density filters. Sold in 2X, 4X, etc. designations, they reduce the light transmission of the lens by one stop, two stops, etc. and demand a corresponding increase in exposure time.

The increase in exposure time can also be useful with ordinary lenses. It has been used to eliminate moving traffic from daylit scenes. Really heavy filtration can bring about so long an exposure that moving objects do not even register on the film. More usefully, an ND filter allows you to adapt a very fast film to bright sunlight shooting. Normally, you would be confined in those circumstances to working at small apertures, perhaps with much more depth of field than you want. By reducing the light transmission, you can shoot at wider apertures and regain the required depth of field control.

Special constructions

Filters were originally introduced for corrective purposes. Early films left a lot to be desired in accurate colour rendering. It did not take long, however, for photographers to realize their creative value, particularly in colour photography, where various effects can be obtained by juggling with colours and image quality. Heavy filtration can render images in monotone or close to it. Couple that with image modification techniques and the possibilities begin to show. As always, there is a danger of overdoing it, but interesting and valid effects can be created.

There are some filters and filter systems that are designed with such creative work in mind. One type is a special construction containing a fixed-position colour filter bonded to a polarizer, and a rotatable polarizing screen. As one polarizer is rotated relative to the other, light transmission is changed to vary the density of the filter. Thus it appears to become of a lighter or darker hue, by merely reducing the amount of light reaching the filter. It is necessary, however, to increase the exposure time or use a wider aperture to obtain a correctly exposed film. These filters are for black-and-white photography only and are available in six colours at a price a great deal higher than that of ordinary filters.

A variation primarily for colour photography may have a little more validity. This, too, works by polarization but it seems to use narrow cut filters of the complementary colours to leave only two of the three primary colours to pass through the construction.

The relative content of these two colours can be varied to give an overall subject illumination between, for example, red and blue. At the same time, the polarizers can work on reflections, and the interesting part is that the reflections are coloured at one extreme or the other of the colour range according to their plane of polarization. Turn the polarizer or the camera and the colour of the reflections is reversed. Various odd effects can be obtained but trial and error seems to be the recommended method of obtaining either effect or exposure.

A less dramatic but perhaps more often usable effect is obtained from partial filters. These, too, are rotating types allowing the filter to affect only part of the scene but they include neutral density to give shaded colours that are peculiarly attractive. The colour effect is not drastic and the filters are available in relatively subdued colours.

Double polarizers are another effect filter that can have valid uses, but more commonly in movie work than in still. A double polarizer, allowing one to be rotated in relation to the other has the effect of absorbing light in a smoothly controllable fashion. They are therefore useful to introduce fade-out and fade-in effects with movie cameras. They can be used for still photography in a similar manner to neutral density filters, with the advantage that only one is needed for a range of densities.

Most of these effects are obtained by combinations of filters and it is surprising that it took so long to come up with a system that made it possible to combine orthodox filters and many others in a single unit. This has now been done by using the existing lens filter thread merely to attach an auxiliary filter holder that can accommodate two filters or screens and allow them to be moved independently.

The filter holder can be attached to any lens with a 49, 52, 55 or

58 mm thread. The special filters designed to go with it compare very favourably in price with normal filters, many of them being much cheaper, and the range at one's disposal is truly extensive. The effects that can be created are so numerous that there is no space to describe or even indicate all of them here.

Naturally, the normal range of filters for black-and-white and colour photography are available, together with starburst, multiple image, diffusion, fog effect and polarizing attachments and many others. There are mask attachments for combination printing, frame masks and an extraordinary 'linear shutter' allowing you to produce elongated, misshappen pictures over two or three film frames.

The filter holder has two slots in which filters can be rotated and moved up and down. The filter holder itself also rotates on its mount so that virtually any filter and screen combination can be created.

Choosing filters

When you first buy your camera, there is no need to quiz the shop assistant on the necessary filters. None is necessary but he may very well try to to sell you at least a UV filter 'to protect your lens'. It might do that, but a dirty filter has more effect on image quality than a dirty lens.

As you begin to take photographs, the need for one or two filters may emerge. A haze or skylight filter certainly has occasional uses. If you do much landscape photography in black-and-white you may well want to have a yellow filter handy on occasions to emphasize a cloud effect. Architecture, more often the steel and concrete type, can sometimes be made more dramatic by overdarkening the sky with an orange or even red filter.

The reddish colour of tungsten lighting could make lips a little pale and a weak green filter might improve matters. But it might also emphasize skin blemishes. Make-up is a better solution.

If you go on to specialize, filters are a help in some cases and almost essential in others. Really careful colour correction can be necessary in catalogue work. Often, you can reproduce a particular limited range of colours almost perfectly, but have to sacrifice

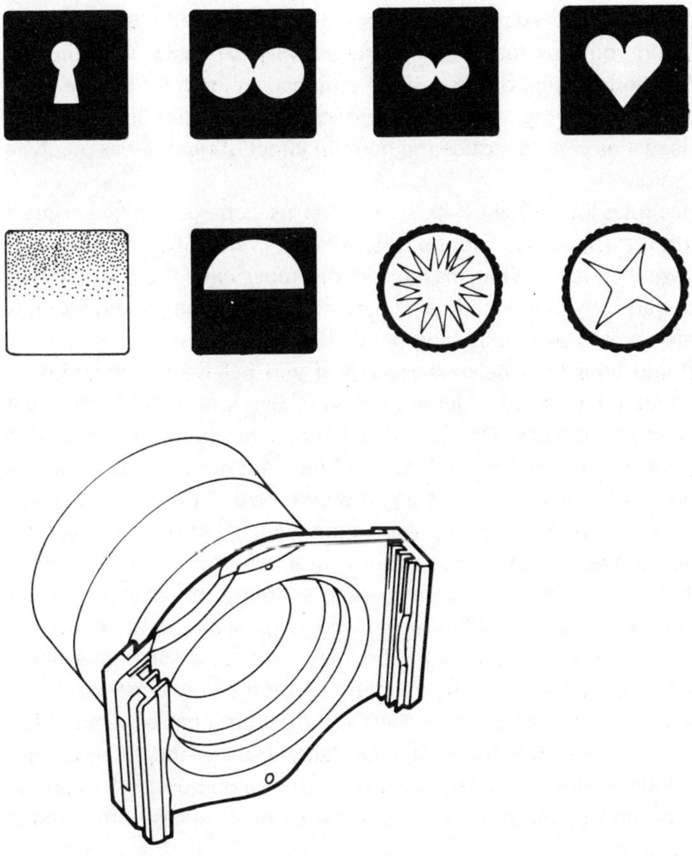

A proprietary filter system depending on an attachment for the lens (*bottom*) into which filters, screens and masks can be slotted. Two filters, screens, etc can be used simultaneously.

others. Sometimes you might falsify colours deliberately, as in some medical work where the actual colours are unimportant but the clear rendering of some features is essential.

When you reach that stage, you need a very clear understanding of all principles involved and a collection of filters specially designed for this type of work. You need to study something like the *Focalguide to Filters,* with its more specialized information.

Buying the filter or filters of your choice involves a judgment of quality and a knowledge of the fitting required. What quality should you look for? You may have a very expensive lens capable of superb definition and high contrast, coated to reduce flare caused by internal reflections, and 'colour-corrected' to perfection. It is just as well to reduce the harmful effect of the filter as much as possible.

That rules out buying filters from the used bargain box—at least without the most minute inspection. Preferably get the best possible quality. That may mean the most expensive—excluding the generally overpriced camera manufacturer's brand—but there is little point in pennypinching here.

Should your filter be multicoated? If you believe implicitly in the multicoating of your lens then you will not want two more reflecting surfaces. On the other hand, what is the effect of two different multicoating techniques? There are no clear-cut answers, possibly because it is not easy to prove them. A good quality filter, coated or not, should have only a marginal effect on the quality of your image. It should not show up too often but flare and extra fall-off could become evident when shooting into the light, or at large apertures. The filter is flat and is generally right out at the front edge of the lens, so there may be a case for a lens hood. Conceivably that could be a better answer than multicoating.

Most filters are supplied in circular form with a male-threaded rim to screw into the front of your lens. That is the filter thread, sometimes marked on the lens rim, usually quoted in the camera instruction book, and measurable on modern lenses with reasonable care.

There have been many threads over the years but modern lenses tend to use a reasonably wide-spaced standard range; the most popular sizes in which are, in millimetres, 49, 52, 55, 58 and 62.

That is the internal diameter of the thread on the lens. There were intermediate sizes, however, and if you have any difficulty in determining your thread size, take the camera to a dealer and get it confirmed.

Lenses for non-reflex cameras are frequently smaller and 40.5 mm has been a popular size. Some of them, and some older lenses, have no filter thread. For those a push-on or clamp-on fitting may be needed. Again, take the camera to a dealer and try whatever fittings he offers before paying any money.

Other Attachments for Lenses

The filter thread of a lens accommodates not only filters but a variety of other attachments that can be screwed into this useful thread. One of the most notable is the close-up or supplementary lens, but that is dealt with in a separate chapter on close-up equipment.

Effects lenses and screens

One of the earliest of the 'special effect' attachments for lenses was a so-called soft-focus lens. It was fashionable at one time, particularly in formal portaiture and movie work, to subdue the occasional cruel sharpness of the camera lens. It was thought unkind to emphasize lines, creases or other skin blemishes. It is possible of course, to slightly defocus the lens so that tiny lines and marks are not resolved but the result is simply an out-of-focus picture.

The habit arose, therefore, of putting something in front of the lens to effect a slight scattering of the light rays before the lens could do its cruel work. This effectively obscured fine detail, particularly the sharp edges between masses of different tone, by spreading the lighter tone into the darker. Small marks disappeared and shadow edges were softened, but the picture was still essentially sharp. The effect came to be known as soft-focus and the attachment as a soft-focus lens.

A soft-focus lens can be created in various ways, the simplest being to engrave concentric lines in a disc of glass placed in front of the lens. If the central area of such a disc is left clear, the degree of softening can be controlled by the lens diaphragm. A wide aperture uses most of the softening rings. A very small aperture might use none of them.

A similar effect can be obtained merely be spreading a thin layer of petroleum jelly over a UV filter or other clear glass disc. At the other extreme there were camera lenses specially made for soft-focus effects. A common practice was to insert a perforated screen in the lens, again with a 'hole' in the middle so that the effect could be controlled by the aperture setting.

The soft-focus lens is not now so popular, most photographers seeming to prefer low-contrast lighting or deliberately-induced flare, but other types of effect attachment developed from it. Probably the most popular, and therefore the most over-used, is the starburst type. A pattern of lines engraved at right angles on the disc instead of concentrically has little effect as a softener but causes small highlights to take on the long streaks of stylistic stars. A square grid gives four points. Put in an extra line to cut the squares into triangles and you get six points. A later development for colour work contains a very large number of lines that use diffraction effects to produce coloured patterns in small highlight areas. Starburst effects can add appeal to some subjects, particularly night shots in wet weather, disco-type lighting and so on. Over-use can soon nullify the effect, however.

Rather more elaborate is the multi-image lens—a faceted lens ground with various faces at different angles instead of one smooth curve. The result is a number of different images of the subject blending one into another. There are many types of multi-image lens, with the images varying in number and pattern. The effect can be striking in movie work for mood creation, continuity breaks, publicity shots, etc. but the applications in still camera work are limited.

The simpler attachments of this type are not too expensive but the faceted types cost rather more than they are really worth, especially in the larger sizes. Consider how many pictures you are likely to make with this type of lens. It is worth taking a long, cool look at its real value to you before rushing off to buy an effect lens. You can't put too many starburst or multiple images all over your pictures, as special effects soon become monotonous.

Auxiliary lenses

There are some more ambitious front-of-lens attachments about which you should be even more cautious. We have already remarked that auxiliary lenses for wide-angle and telephoto effects that fit to the front of the lens are of doubtful value. Nevertheless, there are still a few on sale and they tend to be very expensive for what they offer. They range from very wide-angle types to wide-angle plus close-up, and wide-angle plus telephoto zooms. They often claim edge-to-edge sharpness, which is virtually impossible except at very small apertures and with absolutely first-class prime lenses. If you are tempted to buy one of these attachments, try to get it on a trial basis first. Except with the extreme wide-angle types, which do not claim optical perfection, the change in angle of view is generally so limited that it is hardly worth while.

Most of these auxiliary lenses are suitable only for reflex or other screen-focusing cameras, because they do not include separate viewfinders or focusing scales. This is the very type of camera that does not need them, however, because the much more efficient, behind-the-lens tele-extender can offer a greater magnification, and often at a lower cost.

There is no behind-the-lens wide-angle attachment but, again, some of these attachments are offered at a price that would buy a reasonable wide-angle lens of far greater versatility—and even more so on the used equipment market.

There is one exception to these strictures about front of lens attachments—the monocular. A genuine photographic monocular, and there are one or two, can give surprisingly good results. It attaches to the filter thread of the camera lens and multiplies its focal length by the power of the monocular. An 8 × 30 monocular therefore, converts your 50 mm lens to a 400 mm.

As always, there is a drawback. The front glass is only 30 mm in diameter so the maximum possible aperture is *f*13. In practice, light losses are likely to make it *f*16 or even smaller. Additionally, you can use the monocular for its normal distance-viewing purposes.

Round-the-corner pictures

One front-of-lens attachment that has had a lasting appeal is the mirror box arrangement that allows you to shoot at right angles to your line of sight when looking normally through the camera

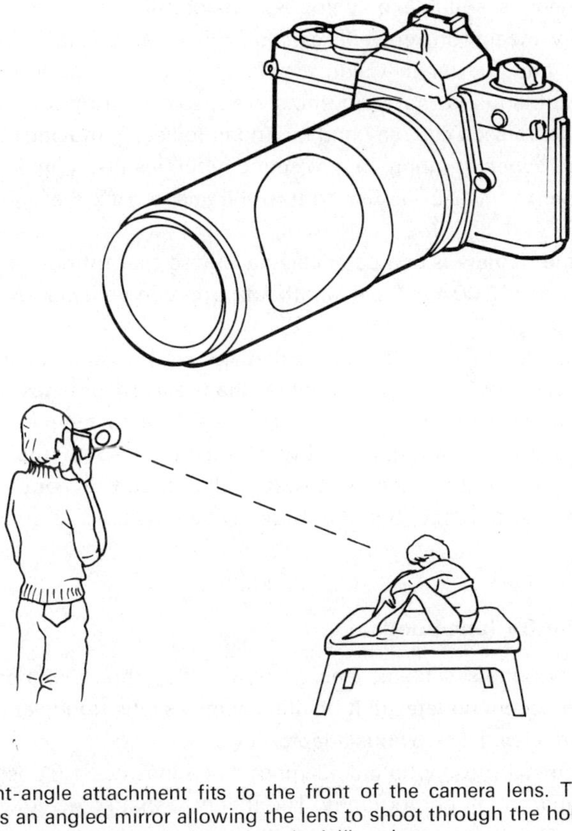

A right-angle attachment fits to the front of the camera lens. The tube houses an angled mirror allowing the lens to shoot through the hole in the side. The front of the tube is made to look like a lens.

eyepiece. It consists of a tube made to look like a lens but with a large opening in one side to throw the image onto a mirror and thence to the camera lens.

It has great appeal for the photographer who is wary of his subject's reaction to being photographed, or for the chronically shy. He can appear to be shooting in a different direction and hope that his subject does not notice the strange hole backed by a mirror in the side of his lens. It has some limited use also for unobserved shooting by allowing just the attachment to protrude past a wall or for periscope-type shooting in crowds.

The disadvantages are important but not crippling Naturally, the attachment is suitable only for screen-focusing cameras, which generally means 35 mm reflexes. You must be able to frame the subject, and the direct-vision viewfinder cannot cope with that. Equally obvious is that your shots are made via a mirror and are laterally reversed. You may find it difficult to keep a moving subject in view. When printing or projecting your results, you have to remember to reverse the film to turn the image back the right way round.

The angle of view is comparatively narrow so that for normal work only lenses of 100 mm focal length and over can be used for a full-frame image.

This attachment is moderately expensive and, again, do not be carried away by the apparent, rather than real, advantages. If you are completely unable to shoot strangers face to face, *and* you expect to do a lot of that type of work, then this gadget might help you. It is one of those things, however, that often turns out to be a good idea at the time, but subsequently languishes in a cupboard unused.

The case for lens hoods

Apart from filters, screens, lenses, etc. the filter thread of a camera lens can accommodate such obvious items as lens hoods and lens caps and a few less obvious adapter rings.

There are still those who are adamant that a lens hood (sunshade) is essential for all photography. The theory is that some light from outside the picture area passes through the front glass and, because it cannot be bent back (refracted) sufficiently to form an image, bounces about inside the lens, taking advantage of all reflective surfaces therein to reach the film eventually as non-image-forming light or flare. So it does, but in most modern lenses, anti-reflection coating and internal baffling reduces the effect to a minimum. Whether it is desirable to reduce it even further is debatable. Super-efficient flare treatment can cause a lens to produce almost unmanageably contrasty images. This is fine for process lenses used in the graphic arts but it can sometimes be too much of a good thing in general photography.

The flare inherent in every lens can be regarded as a valid function. It does no more harm than to reduce contrast. Its total elimination would, in fact, reduce the speed of the lens—or film, whichever way you look at it. It would reduce shadow detail, and that is where true speed lies.

Apart from the effect of the anti-reflection coating, many lenses are protected from flare to some extent by being deeply recessed in their barrels. Not much light reaches them from outside the picture area. There are still many lenses, however, particularly wide-angle types, with large front elements protected by no more than a narrow bezel or rim. These can be subject to flare in certain cirumstances and it is worth trying the effect of a lens hood on them. The snag is that the wider the angle, the smaller and less efficient the lens hood becomes. A fisheye lens obviously cannot have a lens hood.

There is no lens hood that allows only image-forming light to reach the lens in all circumstances. To do that it would need to be tailored to every lens and to every focused distance, not to mention the format. Various types of 'professional' hood are available but it is doubtful whether they are any more efficient in most circumstances than the normal tubular type.

A lens hood must at least be designed for the focal length of the lens. A 25 mm long hood on a lens with a 2° angle of view would be pointless. A 75 mm long hood on a lens with a 90° angle would certainly stop non-image-forming light but would produce a rather small circular image.

It is a matter of personal conviction and the shooting conditions, whether or not you use a lens hood. With bright lights just outside the picture area and a lens you know to be subject to flare, a lens hood is evidently desirable, and you should always use a lens hood with such a lens. In normal conditions, especially with modern lenses, its value is questionable.

Despite that, a lens hood is a wise investment. A camera lens, particularly a large or long lens, is vulnerable to knocks and bangs as the camera is carried around. Its front surface also has an extraordinary magnetic effect on fingers. A lens hood provides very good protection against such mishaps and makes a lot more sense than a UV filter.

The case for caps

A lens cap is a wholly protective device, normally for the lens, occasionally for the meter circuit to avoid drain on batteries. It is wise always to attach a cap to a lens when it is not in use, even if it is stored in its case or a plastic bag. We might as well include the rear lens cap here too. That often serves to project pins and levers in the back of the lens as well as its function of keeping out dust and moisture. It should always be firmly attached when the lens is off the camera.

There are different opinions about front lens caps. On non-reflex cameras they are a nuisance at best and a disaster at worst. It is so easy to forget to remove the cap when you shoot unless you invariably use it and its removal becomes a habit. No such problem arises with reflex cameras and the habitual use of a cap makes sense. The trouble is that, after removing it for a prolonged shooting spell, you may forget where you put it. Then there is the question of the type of lens cap—screw, bayonet, push on, edge-catch, etc. The screw-type is the most secure but is fiddly. The genuine bayonet-type is rare and can also be awkward to use. Push-on types and some of those with push-in edge catches can easily be knocked off. The easiest, but most undesirable, answer is to forget about it. If you do decide to do without a lens cap, think of a hood, because lenses do need protection in use and while carrying them about.

Adapter rings

There are three main types of adapter ring for lens filter threads—coupling, reversing and stepping.

A coupling ring allows two lenses to be joined together by their filter threads. It has two male threads. The purpose of this is to allow a standard focal length camera lens to be used as a powerful supplementary lens when placed in front of a telephoto lens on the camera. This subject is dealt with more fully in the chapter on close-up equipment.

A reversing ring allows a lens to be mounted in reverse on the camera or on an accessory such as bellows or extension tubes. It has a male filter thread and a male lens thread or bayonet to suit the particular camera system. In practice, very close-range photography can often be carried out in this way without either tubes or bellows. Many lenses are deeply recessed in their barrels and are therefore well forward of the infinity position when reversed directly on the camera. They then have only one focused distance, however, except in some later lenses with internal focusing. On normal-focusing lenses operating the focusing ring can draw the lens into its mount to provide a degree of hooding.

A stepping ring converts the lens filter thread from one size to another. With lenses of two different sizes, you can buy a stepping ring to allow one size of filter to be used on both lenses. The adapter may be a step-up or step-down ring. A 58-62 mm adapter is a step-up type, allowing a 62 mm filter to be used on a lens with a 58 mm filter thread. It has a 58 mm male thread and a 62 mm female and is sometimes listed as M58-F62 to avoid all doubt.

Step-down rings allow smaller filters to be used on larger lenses which, with very large lenses can effect quite a saving in price. Naturally, they are liable to affect the maximum aperture of the lens and you have to conduct a few experiments to determine the extent of the effect. Step-down rings are usually quoted in the form 62-58, etc.

Matte box effects

If your camera has multi-exposure facilities (i.e. you can easily make more than one exposure on the same frame) you can create a variety of special effects with a matte box and a selection of masks. Even without multiple exposures, you can make circular, oval or vignetted pictures directly in the camera.

The matte box is, in effect, a rectangular (usually square) lens hood and can double for that purpose without its attachments. The attachments consist of a mask holder and masks to fit. The masks can be split screen types, allowing you to put a different subject (or the same subject) into each half of the picture, various shapes for insets, banners or flashes, grids, jigsaws, etc. They need some care in use—the focused distance should be the same for each shot to avoid gaps or overlap—and their applications depend a lot on the ingenuity of the operator if the results are not to appear hackneyed. There are various commercial opportunities in wedding, portrait, family group and similar work.

Rear-of-lens attachments

Accessories to fit between the lens and the camera body are, not surprisingly, for interchangeable-lens cameras, but not necessarily only for screen focusing types.

Perhaps the most frequently encountered accessories of this kind are extension tubes and bellows, which are dealt with in the chapter on close-up equipment. The next most popular is the tele-extender or tele-converter.

The principle of the tele-converter is very old indeed. Astronomers used the idea to enlarge telescope images more than a century ago and it was subsequently adapted to cameras to provide the special telephoto construction.

A tele-converter is a negative (diverging) lens, unlike the positive (converging) lens on the camera. It works by lessening the convergence of the camera lens so that its image is focused further back. That in itself results in a larger image so the film receives only part of the image produced by the camera lens but on a larger scale. The converter is of such a length that the image is focused correctly on the film for the distance indicated by the focusing scale. That, incidentally, makes the converter usable on non-reflex cameras and makes it possible to couple it with a rangefinder. Most versions provide a doubling of focal length but 1.4X, 3X, 2 and 3X, and 2-3X zoom types are also available.

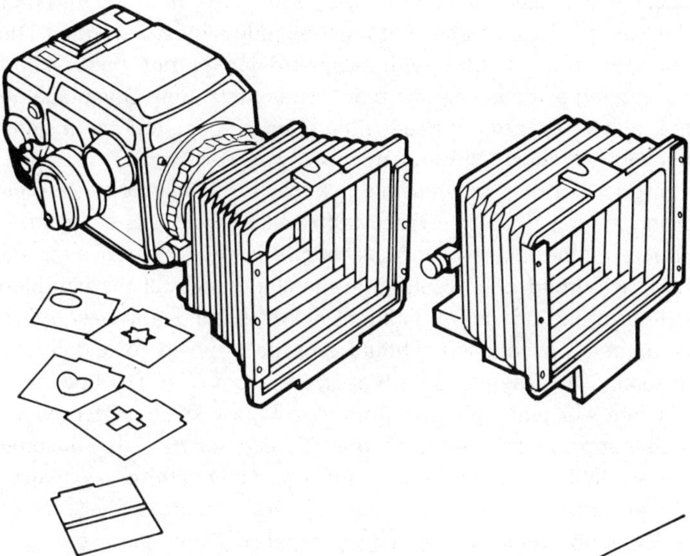

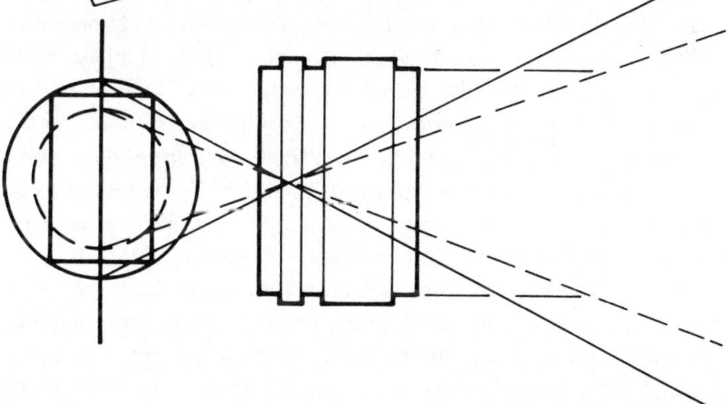

A matte box, also known as an effects box, available in 6×6 cm and 35 mm sizes. A wide variety of screens is supplied enabling various vignette, split screen, superimposition and similar effects to be obtained. Alone the box acts as a lens hood.
The effect of too long a lens hood (*bottom*) is shown by the broken line.

A good, modern tele-converter is a useful accessory for those who occasionally need a lens of longer focal length than the maximum they have available, and that must include almost everyone. They are said to work best with telephoto lenses but there is little convincing evidence on that point. The outstanding advantage of a tele-converter is that it needs little storage space but can instantly convert, a modest 135 mm lens to 270 mm or 405 mm.

The price for that convenience is a loss of illumination at the film plane, owing to the increased light path. The loss is equal to the square of the increase in focal length. With a 2X converter, you have a fourfold loss, resulting in the illumination at the film plane falling to one-quarter of its intensity without the converter. All the *f*-numbers on your lens should thus be doubled to restore their accuracy. A 50 mm lens with apertures from *f*2 to *f*16 becomes a 100 mm lens with apertures from *f*4 to *f*32. A 3X converter reduces illumination to one-ninth, so that *f*2 becomes *f*6. Tele-converters are available at various prices and it is fairly safe to say that the cheaper they are, the less likely they are to perform well. On the other hand, some are extremely expensive and there can be a reasonable doubt whether they are really worth that much more than middle of the range types. Certainly some of the earliest kinds were very poor. Now there are not many with fewer than four elements in their construction and a lot with six or more, with a consquent increase in picture quality. There are undoubtedly some that are well worth the cost for occasional use. If you intend to do a lot of work at the extended focal length, however, a not-too-expensive prime lens will almost certainly serve you better.

The only other rear-of-lens attachments, apart from close-up equipment, are lens-mount adapters. There is at present a tentative movement toward a certain amount of standardization in methods of attaching the lens to the camera but it is doubtful whether it can go very far. The Praktica M42 screw gained a lot of followers but is shortly to be deserted by its originators. Asahi have already left it and have managed to license their bayonet to a few other manufacturers but it is unlikely that the famous names will change their established designs in the cause of standardization. As electronic control is extended such a move should be possible and would be of undoubted consumer benefit but would not serve the

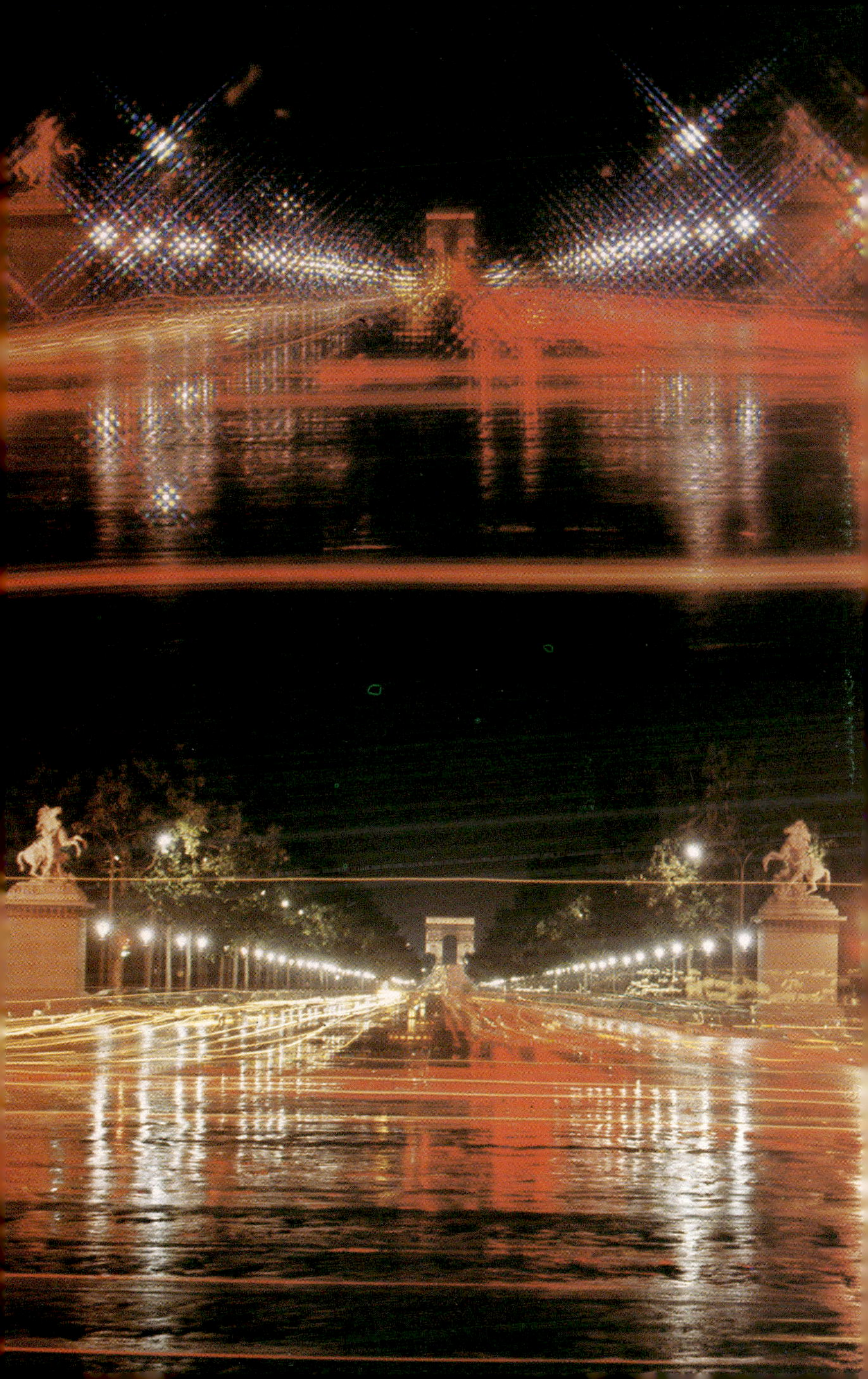

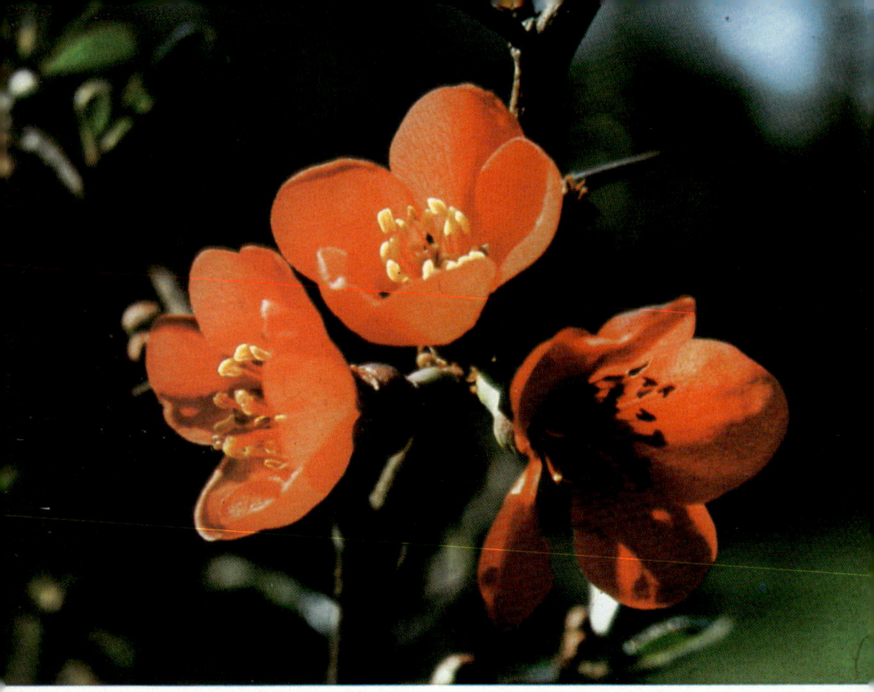

Above A useful accessory is the zoom close-up lens attachment which not only provides intermediate degrees of magnification over the usual fixed close-up lenses but also has a longer dioptric range. *Raymond Lea*

Opposite, top A copy made from a sandwich of two transparencies photographed with the aid of zoom close-up lens. *Raymond Lea*
Opposite, bottom Impact can be added by copying a transparency through a red filter *Raymond Lea*

Previous page, top A long exposure through a 'star burst' attachment. This is engraved with a pattern of lines at right angles and causes small highlights to take on streaks of stylistic stars.
Previous page, bottom The same scene but taken without the attachment. The horizontal streaks are from moving car lights passing during the exposure.
Sidney Ray

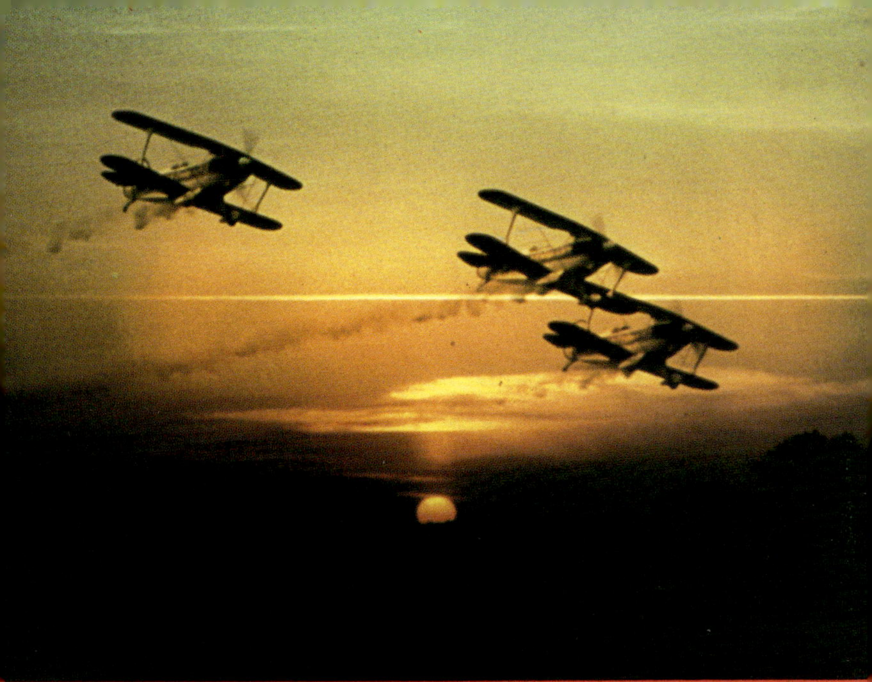

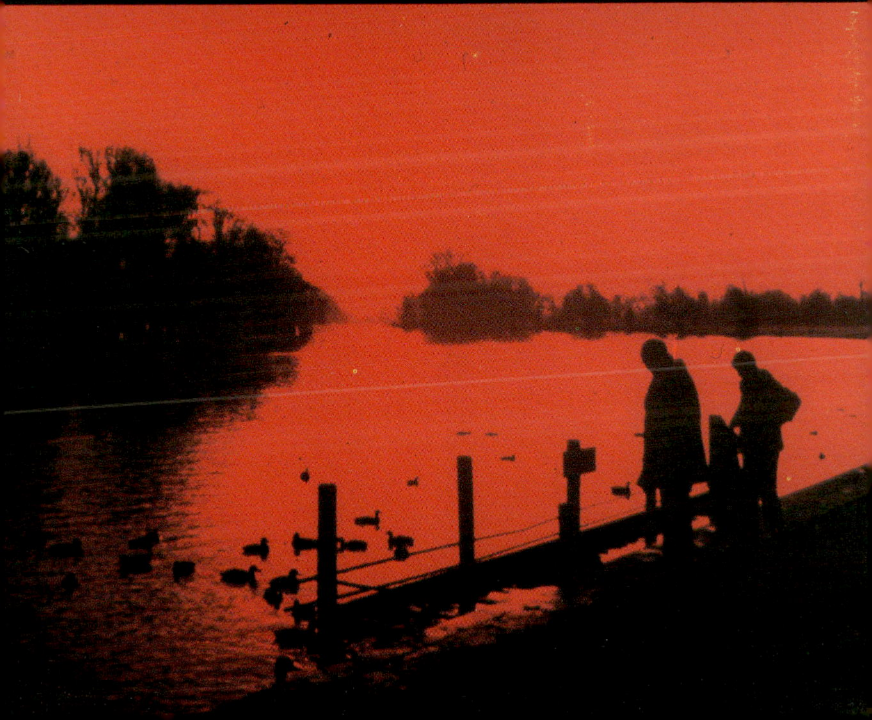

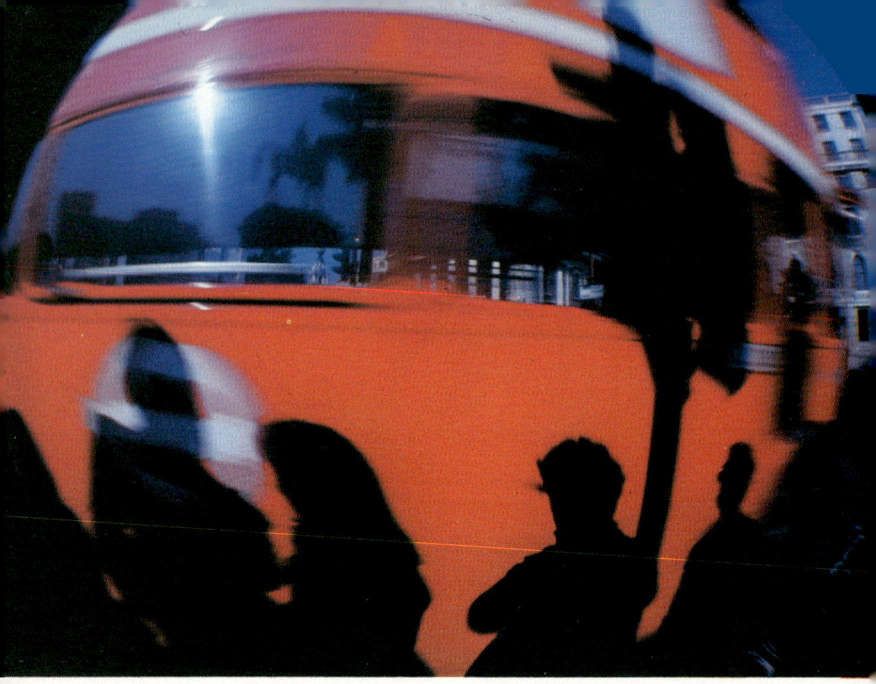

The image from a fisheye lens is now quite familiar. Fisheye lenses are expensive but relatively inexpensive attachments are available and results are perfectly acceptable when used with a good quality lens. *Sidney Ray*

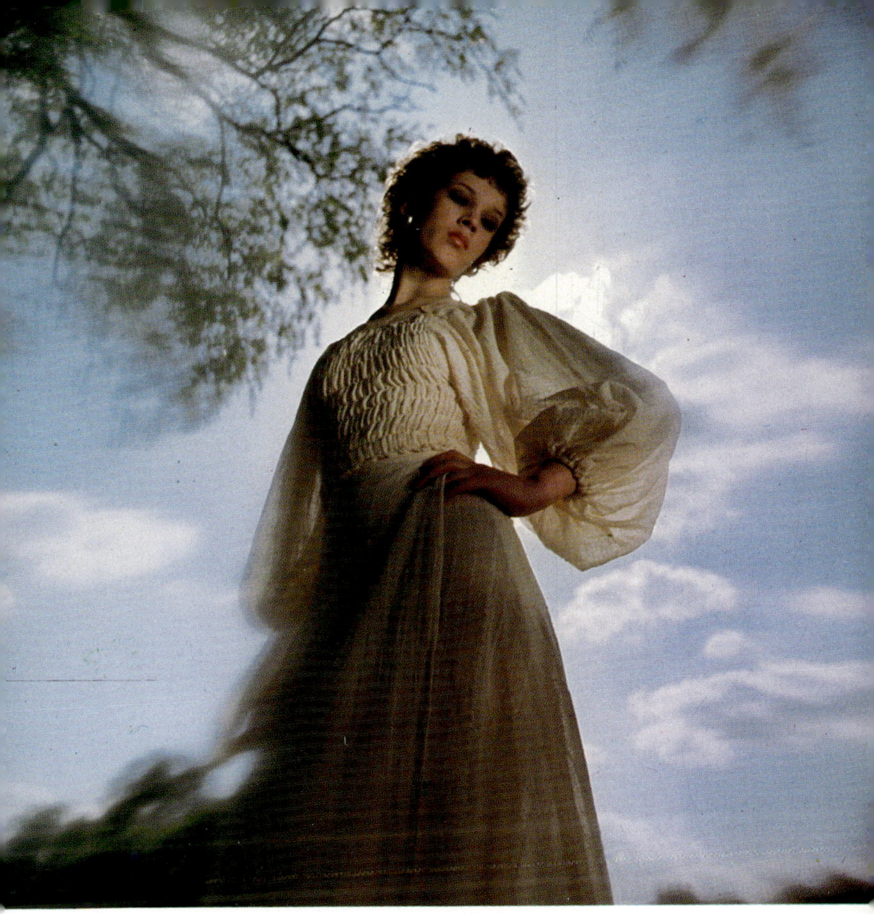

An attractive soft-focus effect is achieved by fitting an ultraviolet filter over the lens and coating with a thin layer of petroleum jelly. A clear central area is left untreated. *Michael Barrington-Martin*

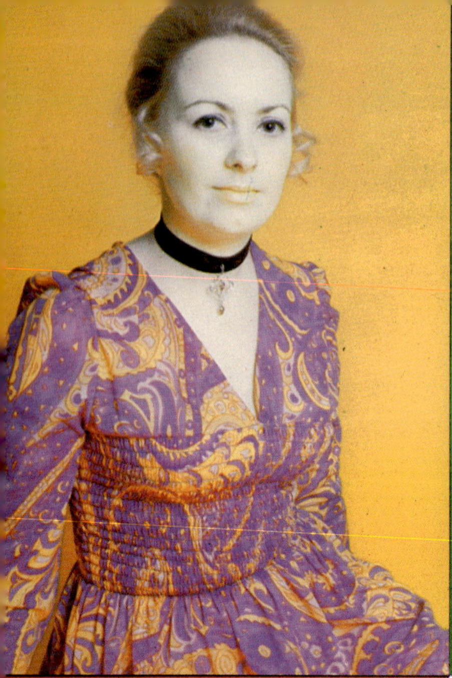
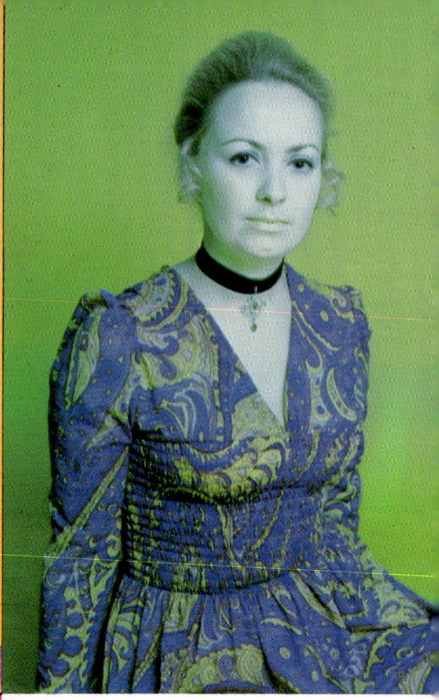
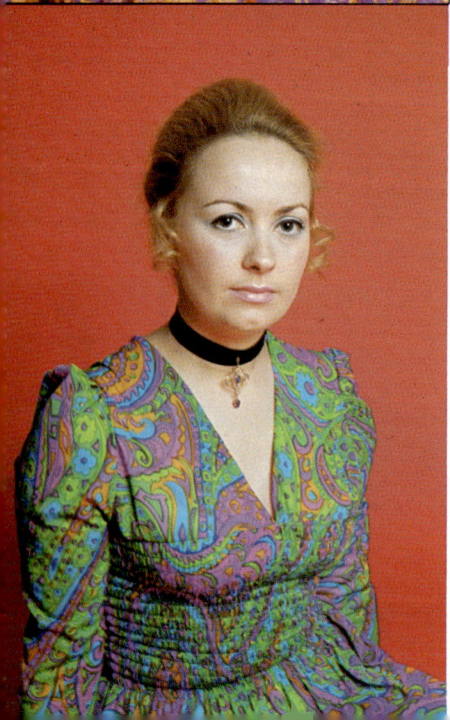

Infrared-sensitive film produces false colours and gives your pictures a new look. A normal subject *(left)* is transformed with Infrared Ektachrome through the recommended Wratten 12 filter *(above, left)*. Removing the IR by adding a second filter (Chance ON22) changes the colours yet again *(above, right)*. *Sidney Ray*

Opposite The four pictures show the effects of using a polarizing filter with different colour films. Top row, left to right, Agfachrome with and without the filter; bottom row, Kodak Ektachrome under the same conditions. *Sidney Ray*

Overleaf Multiple images of the same subject can be made in a single exposure by fitting a multi-facet attachment over the camera lens. Each image is slightly different and the attachment can be rotated to suit composition. *Sidney Ray*

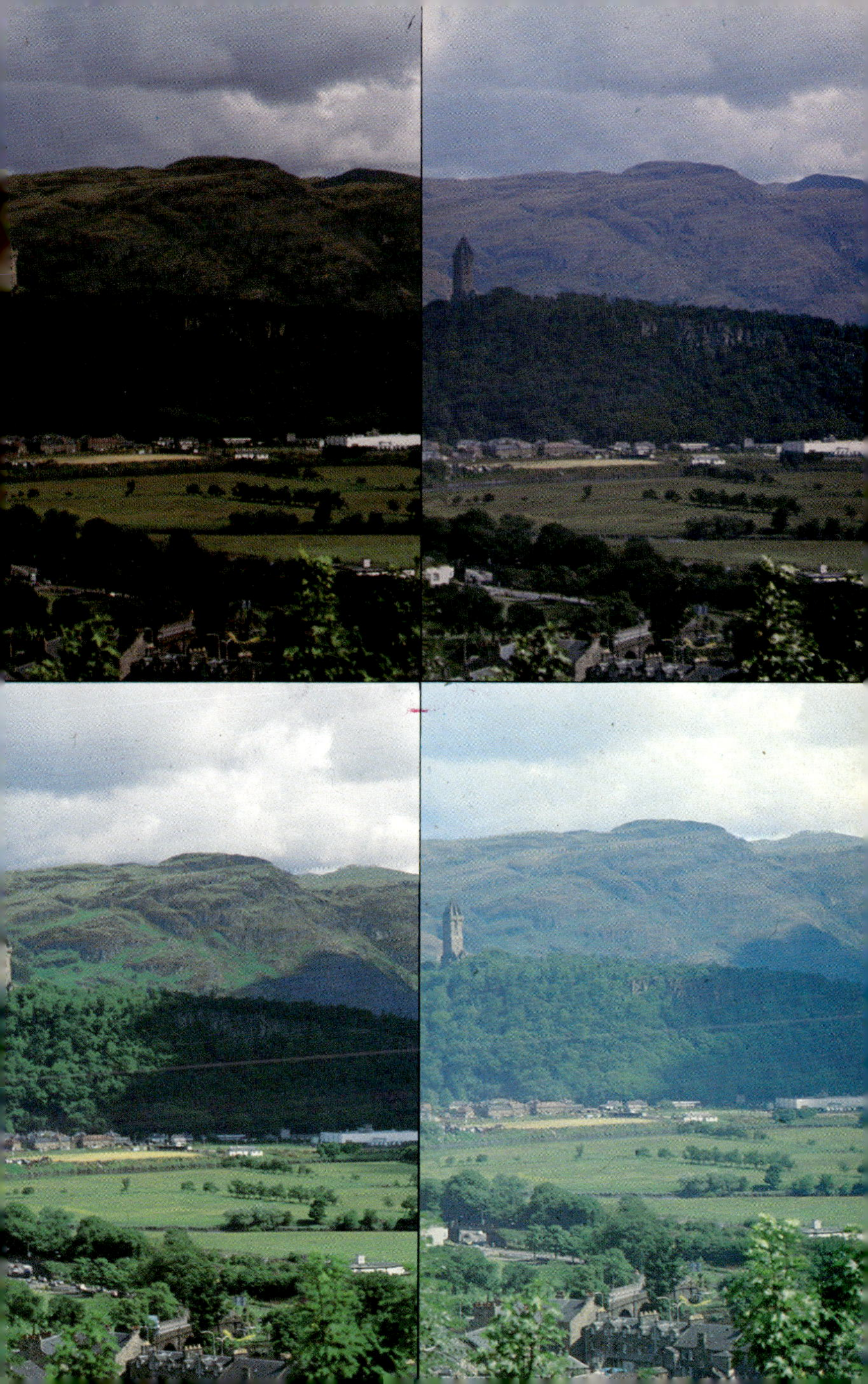

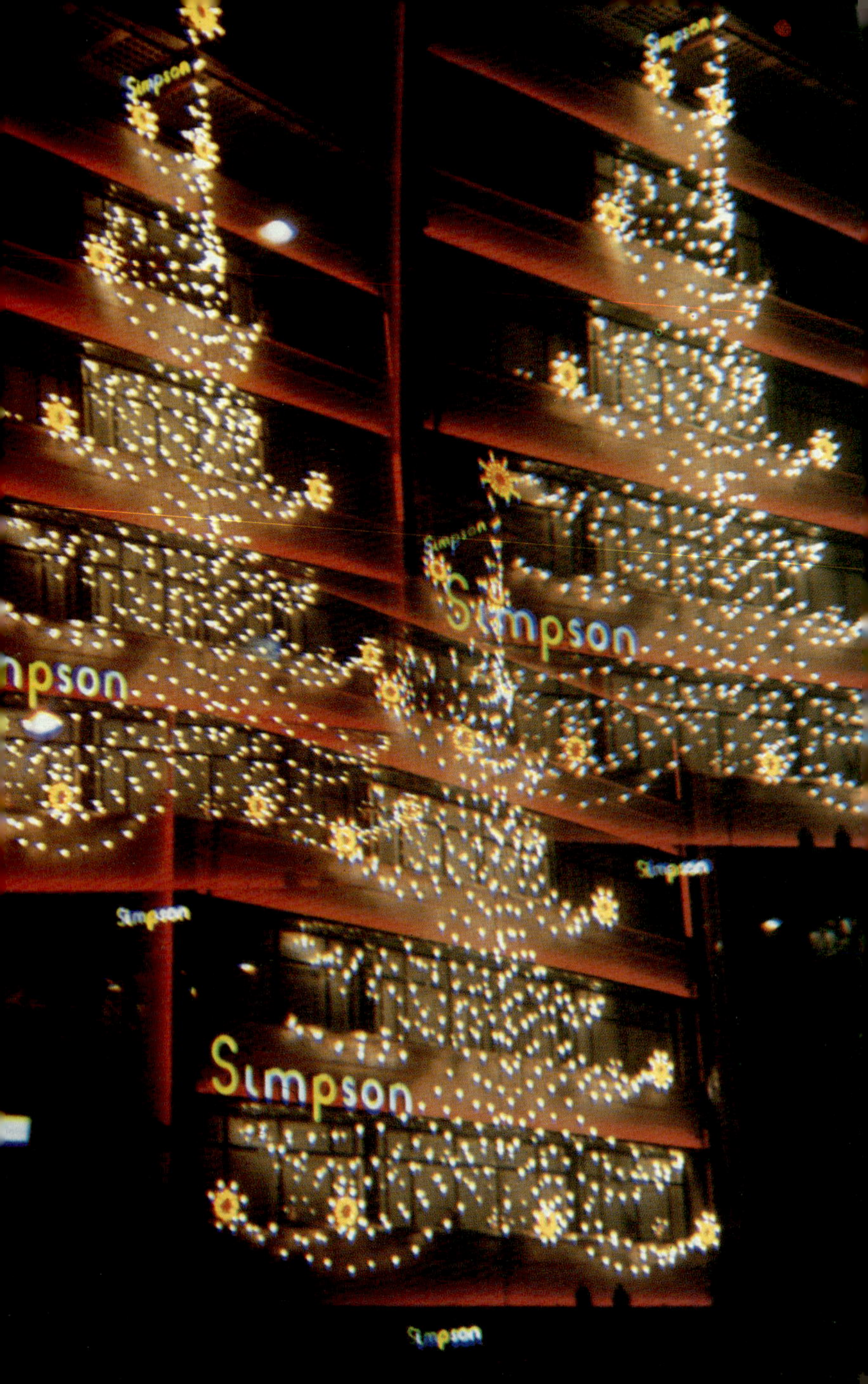
Simpson
Simpson
Simpson
Simpson
Simpson
Simpson

manufacturers' interests. Consequently, except with the many cameras still using the M42 mount, lens attachment methods tend to be unique to each marque. If you change your camera there is the virtual certainty that your lenses will not fit your new model.

Accessory manufacturers do their best to overcome this problem by supplying adapters that can be attached to the rear of your lens and to the new camera. Some independent lens manufacturers supply their lenses in a common mount to which a variety of adapters can be fitted, so that when you change your camera, you change only the adapter and not the whole lens. That can cope with most changes while the adapter that attaches to a complete lens sometimes runs into problems of camera body depth, and lens mount diameter. If one body is considerably deeper than the other, it is unlikely that another lens could be adapted to it except for close-up work. Either method can come unstuck in the matters of auto-diaphragm, full-aperture metering and other more sophisticated lens-to-camera connections. However, most of the better-known interchangeable-mount lenses have mounts which couple with all the functions on popular cameras.

When you think about changing your camera, therefore, or even when you buy your first interchangeable-lens type, and certainly before buying a used model, give some thought to the lens-mounting method. Check the independent lenses to see whether they offer fully compatible types. Make sure that the used camera in particular does not have a unique lens-mounting system no longer in use. Lenses may be very difficult to come by. None of this is very important if you are going to stick with the camera you buy (except for the out-of-date used model) but it can affect its resale value and might make it necessary for you to sell lenses you would rather not part with.

Adapters are available from stock for most popular conversions and even for a few discontinued models. In other cases, it is possible to have adapters made on a one-off basis but they are naturally more expensive. In a few cases the conversion is impossible. Before you order an adapter, make sure you know exactly what it will and will not do. Specify clearly what you want and put the onus on the supplier to tell you whether his product comes up to your specification or not.

Working out the Exposure

As soon as you acquire a camera with more than one or two shutter speeds and lens apertures, you run into exposure problems. The film needs a certain amount of light to produce an image, but you must decide on the camera settings that give just that amount of light—no more, no less.

It is not the function of this book to provide the answers, merely to point the way to where they may be found. There are, of course, a lot of automatic-exposure cameras around now. With most photographic subjects they work extremely well to give you a more or less factual representation of the subject. But this is not always what you want. You may wish to show a backlit subject as a silhouette or as if there were more frontal lighting; you may want to increase or decrease contrast. That is when you feel the need for assistance and information.

Books, charts and tables

Books are photographic accessories, just as lenses and filters are, and a lot of books have been written on the subject of exposure. This is not surprising because correct exposure is vital to the production of technically good pictures. Imaginative or creative photography may use exposure tricks but many photographers have to produce clear, crisp pictures showing every detail of the subject.

Understanding the exposure problem is a great help in solving it, so we can confidently recommend you to read as much as possible about the subject. It *can* be learned, certainly on the technical level, from books, and technical knowledge is at least useful, even if you only want to use exposure as a tool to produce imaginative and individual results. Technically, exposure is a straightforward matter that can be simplified into charts and tables. Given the film sensitivity, the lighting conditions and standard processing, it is a fairly simple matter to calculate a combination of lens aperture and shutter speed that will give correct exposure.

Many tables have been produced on those principles. The simplest is that provided in the instruction leaflet packed with most films. If the film has a sensitivity of 80ASA, for example, you might get something like this:

Bright or Hazy Sun on Light Sand or Snow	Bright or Hazy Sun (Distinct Shadows)	Weak Hazy Sun (Soft Shadows)	Cloudy Bright (No Shadows)	Cloudy Dull or Open Shade†
f/16 1/125 s	*f*/11* 1/125 s	*f*/8 1/125 s	*f*/5.6 1/125 s	*f*/4 1/125 s

In weak hazy sunshine, you set your shutter speed to 1/125 second and your lens aperture to *f*8—or to any equivalent settings, such as 1/250 second and *f*5.6 or 1/60 second and *f*11.

For most subjects you need no more information. After all, no more is supplied to the automatic-exposure camera, which is calibrated to give exposures of that nature when its meter reads light levels corresponding to those in the table.

There are much more elaborate charts available, such as those working on a system of points allotted for geographical position, time of day, nature of subject, film sensitivity, etc. The points are all totted up and the total looked up on a table that indicates shutter speed and/or aperture to be set. The tables are ingenious and they work. They must, because the problem is usually capable of purely mechanical solution. Such tables are, unfortunately, not practical. They help you to understand the principles involved but are a little too cumbersome in the field.

The 'bright or hazy' sun column in the film manufacturer's leaflet is the standard exposure and that works roughly on the principle of using the shutter speed numerically nearest to the film speed figure and an aperture of *f*16, i.e. for 80ASA, 1/60 second at *f*16 or its equivalents. The other columns follow at one stop intervals.

Exposure meter practice

Most photographers, at least in the hobby field, rely totally on the exposure meter built into their cameras. For a few years, in fact, the hand-held separate meter almost fell into disuse as the advantages of the built-in, and particularly the through-the-lens, types were extolled beyond all reason. Of course, built-in meters are an advantage and TTL meters have the slight additional advantage of measuring only the picture area or perhaps even only a part of it, but that is generally all they can do. They take an average, reflected-light reading of what they see and should come up with an answer close to that given by the film manufacturer's leaflet.

Only a few can be used to measure the light reflected from a particular small area of the subject. They cannot easily assess subject or lighting contrast, and are clumsy to take to or around the subject. They are not suitable for incident-light reading and they are rarely of any value to assess negative density or assist with enlarger exposures. The good separate meter can do all these things and more.

Even the most sceptical of us will rarely buy a small format camera without a built-in TTL meter, having become so conditioned to its use. Indeed, we do not often have the choice because there are comparatively few cameras of this type without them. The meter undoubtedly has its uses in day-to-day photography but it does have a tendency to mesmerise you into making constant minor alterations to exposure that can have no possible effect on the result. With a hand-held meter you are much more likely to assess the lighting conditions once and then make your own individual adjustments according to the nature of the subject and the type of result you want.

Types of exposure meter

After briefly almost succumbing to the onslaught of built-in versions, hand-held exposure meters are now available in various forms. There are two important divisions—large-area reading and spot—and three less important—selenium, cadmium sulphide (CdS) and silicon.

Most hand-held meters read an area within about a 30° arc, but there are a few genuine spot meters reading only about a 1° or smaller arc. We shall come to those later.

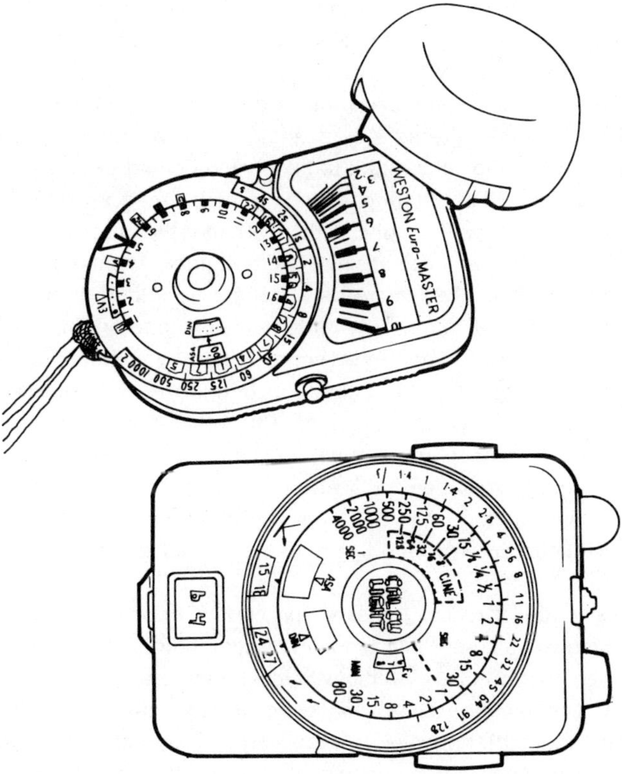

The traditional exposure meter (*top*) uses no battery and gives readings by needle and scale. The latest version is all-electronic with digital readout.

The other division is concerned with the type of light-sensitive material used. An exposure meter works on the principle that certain materials respond electrically to light, either generating a current or changing resistance according to the amount of light they receive. The response can be translated by a sensitive meter and needle or by an electronic circuit to indicate the 'light value' and/or recommended exposures for a pre-set film sensitivity.

Selenium was the first material to come into popular use. Its advantages are its close correlation with the colour sensitivity of panchromatic films and the fact that it generates a current large enough to drive a meter movement. Its disadvantage, compared with later materials, is that it needs to be of a relatively large area to attain usable sensitivity.

Cadmium sulphide came next and looked as if it would totally supersede selenium. It had the advantage of a considerably better size/sensitivity ratio, allowing it to be located behind a camera lens and so provide TTL metering. Selenium cells could be built into cameras but not in the light path. CdS has the disadvantages, however, that it is oversensitive to red light, compared with panchromatic film. Also it needs a battery, is rather sluggish in reaction, and needs time to recover from exposure to bright light.

The oversensitivity to red can be counteracted by including a blue filter in the system but full correction brings the CdS sensitivity down close to that of selenium. The battery is unavoidable because CdS changes its electrical resistance on exposure to light. That changing resistance has to be used to modulate the current supplied by a battery. All in all, it is doubtful whether CdS would ever have been brought into use but for the need to introduce TTL metering.

The next material to be used and the current front runner, was a silicon derivative commonly known as silicon blue—again from the filter fitted to correct its oversensitivity to red. Like selenium, this material generates a current on exposure to light. Unlike both selenium and CdS, however, it reacts very quickly—so quickly that it can be switched by the camera shutter release and activate an electronic circuit before the shutter opens. Although it generates a current, however, silicon blue still needs a battery, because the current is so small that it has to be amplified.

Other materials are used but silicon and selenium are, perhaps, more likely to survive than CdS—at least in hand-held meters. The sluggish reaction of CdS and its need for battery power give it no very great advantage over selenium.

Choosing a meter

The number and variety of hand-held meters is expanding rapidly as demand re-establishes itself and as new designs take advantage of the fast-reacting silicon sensors.

The basic selenium meter is still very much alive—notably as the Weston Euromaster, latest of a long line of renowned meters from the Sangamo Weston factory. Still using a needle and a scale, this is the type of meter that can be used to convey the information needed by practitioners of zone systems of exposure. The selenium meter may not be able to read moonlight but as no meter reading can give you much more than a guess at such low light levels, that is hardly a drawback. The Weston will, after all, give a perfectly reliable reading at 3 m or more from a shaded 100-watt lamp and has the great advantage of not needing a battery.

Most CdS meters give greater sensitivity than the selenium types. They can be made to give quite extreme sensitivity but their sluggish reaction to low light levels makes this a doubtful advantage. They are gradually being replaced by silicon types and, if your need is not urgent, it might be as well to wait until these more efficient versions begin to come down in price.

One great advantage of the silicon meter is its versatility. Its fast reaction enables it to be produced as the core of an exposure meter system. With suitable adapters, it can be used as a flashmeter, colour temperature meter, spot meter, enlarger meter and so on.

The type of reading given by various meters might influence your choice. The traditional meter uses a needle swinging across a scale, which may give you no more than a single exposure recommendation and leave you to work out alternatives for yourself. Sometimes a calculator dial is used, showing all the alternatives at a glance and, as with the Weston, giving alternative index marks for shadow and highlight readings and other information.

The vulnerability of the less-well-made meter movements brought about the introduction of light-emitting diodes (LEDs) as signal lamps in place of the swinging needle. Later developments brought full electronic circuits to give digital readouts. These can also be combined with calculator dials as in one of the latest designs claiming a range of two million to one on a single scale. With this model, you press a button to obtain a two-digit readout instantly convertible to exposure readings on a large calculator dial. Let go of the button and the readout fades. Press it again and a memory circuit recalls the reading. So that the reading can be retained in the memory almost indefinitely, there is no on-off switch. Power consumption, from four 1.5 volt batteries is extremely low.

The choice, therefore, is really between a relatively inexpensive meter for use in conjunction with the camera only, and a much more versatile and expensive type for use in various other circumstances as well. There is very little sense in buying an expensive meter for camera use only on the grounds that it can read the proverbial black cat in a coal cellar. When exposures reach the level of one second or more, the reaction of the film emulsion can become unpredictable without precise information from the film manufacturer. That information is available but the electronic wizards have not yet got round to programming it into their meter circuits.

Spot meters

Some manufacturers claim 'spot' reading for their TTL meters by confining the meter's angle of acceptance to a small part of the picture area. This can be a useful facility only if the photographer fully understands the principles involved, otherwise such a meter can give very unsatisfactory results.

The genuine spot meter is a separate instrument with an angle of acceptance no greater than one degree of arc or less. It allows you to measure the intensity of light in what will be a very small part of your picture area unless you are using a giant long-focus lens. It can be used in the normal exposure meter mode—to measure the light reflected by a mid-tone—but is more often used for shadow

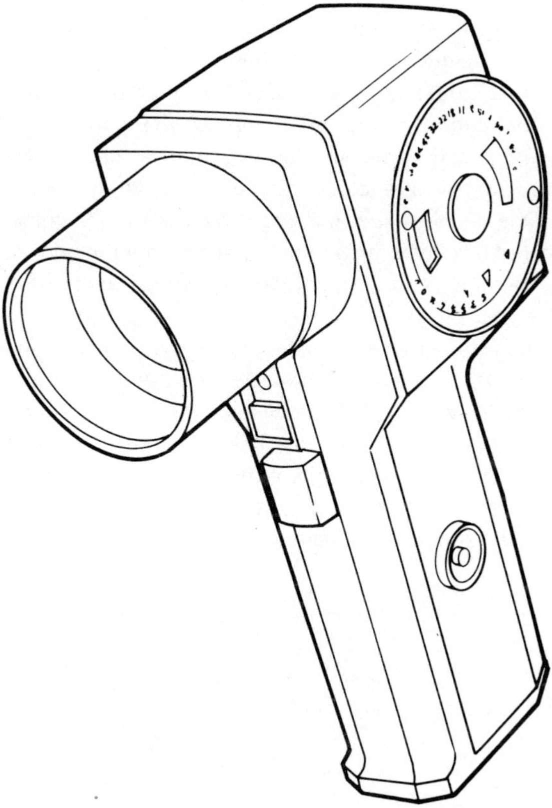

A typical spot meter designed primarily to read over a one-degree angle at relatively long range, but also able to read from very small areas at close range.

or highlight readings, to check the brightness range of the subject. Most photographers take straightforward reflected-light readings of the whole subject area and obtain perfectly exposed results most of the time. They know enough to adjust the reading when it is not likely to provide the result they want. But many photographers specialize in subjects that are commonly of the type that could mislead a meter. Others use a metering system that depends on careful measurements of the brilliance of various parts of the subject.

Colour films have a limited ability to handle great contrasts in lighting. They can reproduce the differences in tone adequately but colour fidelity must suffer at one end of the range or the other. A spot meter can give an indication of the limits, so that the photographer can adjust the lighting or use fill-in from flash or reflectors. Low-lit interiors, as in churches, often have important inaccessible detail. A spot meter can measure the illumination of a small part of a stained glass window and so tell the knowledgeable photographer how it is likely to reproduce with exposures at various levels.

Spot meters are expensive instruments and their uses are highly specialized. The average photographer has no use for them. He can cope perfectly well with an ordinary meter and a good understanding of the basics. Those who take exposure very seriously and intend to pursue to the full one of the 'zone' systems can hardly do without a spot meter—if only to avoid buying an extremely expensive densitometer to read negative densities.

Aids to Viewing and Focusing

Most cameras have an eyepiece. There are, of course, direct focusing screen types for use in studios and for technical work and a few reflexes that are not generally used at eye level but the mass market camera is a hand-held, eye-level type of various designs.

The eyepiece of a non-reflex camera cannot usefully be added to or modified in any way, except as may occasionally be provided by a built-in mechanism. In some such cameras, for example, the field of view through the eyepiece alters as you change lenses. More commonly, however, when you change the lens, you also change the viewfinder.

Viewfinder for non-reflexes

The additional viewfinder clips into the accessory shoe on the camera top plate and you use the rangefinder, where fitted, in the normal viewfinder. Auxiliary finders come in various forms. They may be single types for one focal length only, or in a small turret form, tiny lenses rotating on a disc to give the appropriate field of view for the lens in use. A third type looks rather like a single viewfinder but has a zoom-type adjustment allowing it to cover several focal lengths.

Attachable viewfinders have taken many forms over the years but few of them are still available as separate items, except on the used market. They can be useful with those older cameras that have rather unsatisfactory viewfinding systems.

Brightline finders were very popular. They used the old Albada system which had a partially silvered curved glass at the front and a frame printed on the the rear glass. The effect as you looked through the eyepiece was of a frame apparently suspended in the same plane as the image of the subject. Brightlines were simply updated Albadas giving a brighter, larger image and frame. The advantages of the system were the clear delineation of the frame (the edges of the ordinary viewfinder frame are not always so clear) and the fact that the frame was within the viewing area. Parts of the subject just outside the picture area could be seen.

A similar type also used the suspended frame idea but in a vastly different way. The large eyepiece was a lens focused on a frame etched into a black glass at the front, effectively putting the frame out at some distance from the eye. The black glass obscured all except the frame so the other eye was kept open to view the scene. It takes a little getting used to but has all the advantages of the brightline finder, together with a life-size image and two-eyed viewing. Naturally, there is no loss of illumination and you can watch moving objects come into shot from a long way out.

These finders were essentially for single focal lengths. They incorporated parallax marks to compensate for their distance from the lens in close-range work; or, occasionally, a primitive form of parallax adjustment that allowed the viewfinder to be tilted downward.

There were also various types of metal frame finders, consisting of an eyepiece aperture spaced at a fixed distance behind an open frame according to the focal length of the lens. This was a common type of 'sports finder' on screen focusing cameras that could also be hand-held but a few stouter models were made to fit into an accessory shoe. They are not noted for accuracy but are better than nothing if you have an old camera with only the tiny reflex finder fitted to most early models.

Brightline and turret finders are still available for 35 mm interchangeable-lens non-reflexes but the other types are rare. There may be some available with specialized equipment but they are not on general sale.

Most current viewing aids are for screen focusing or reflex cameras. In these cameras, you see the image projected on a screen by the camera lens and it is an easy matter to modify the eyepiece to suit the view of the image to particular conditions.

Eyesight correction lenses

You view the image on the screen of an SLR camera through a

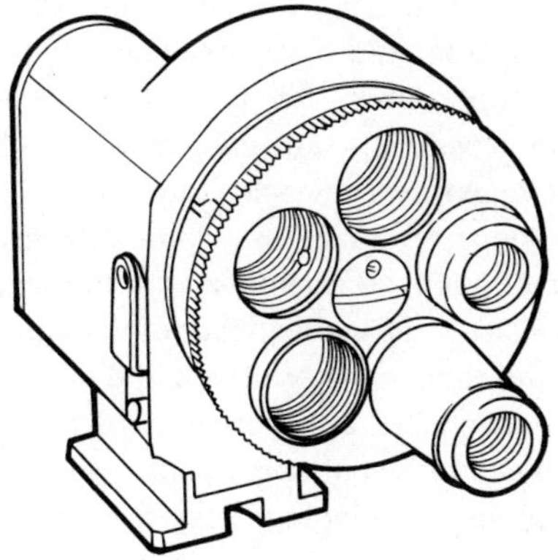

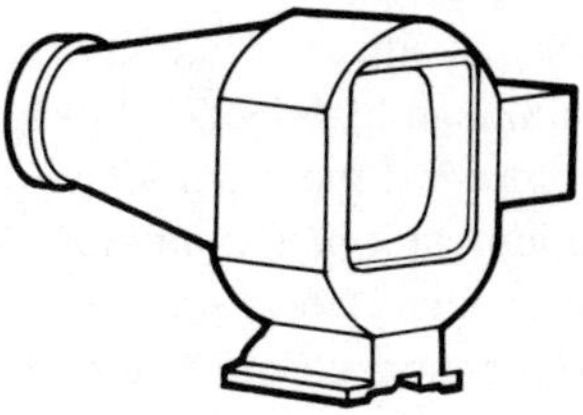

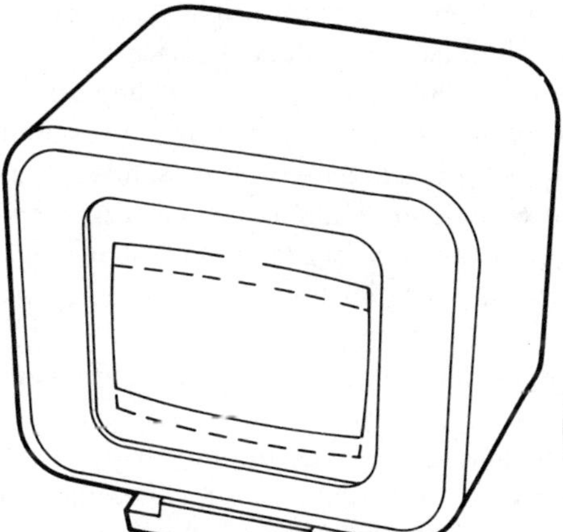

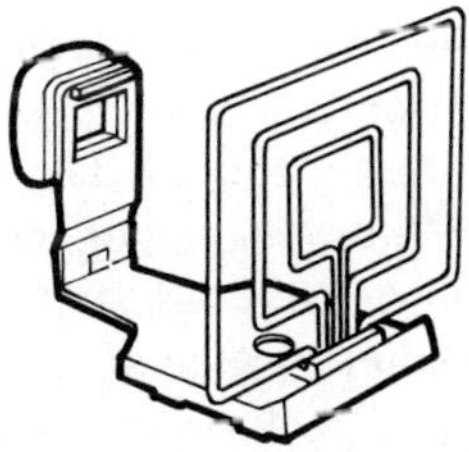

The turret viewfinder (*top left*) is still occasionally supplied for non-reflex interchangeable-lens cameras. Individual viewfinders for each lens are otherwise necessary (*top right*) and are sometimes required for very wide-angle lenses on SLRs. The Kontur finder (*bottom left*) had to be used with both eyes open. The open frame finder is popular for action photography.

fixed-focus eyepiece, because your eye is too close to the image to be able to focus it unaided. The focal length of the eyepiece is such that it works as a sort of supplementary lens to allow the eye to focus at the screen distance. It works adequately for most people, despite variations in eyesight, provided those with significantly defective eyesight wear their spectacles to view.

If you find that your viewfinder image is fuzzy, ask somebody else to look at it first, preferably somebody who is familiar with the type of camera. Don't judge by the clarity of any exposure indicators, shutter speed figures, etc. that may appear in, or beside, the field of view because they could effectively be at a different distance. When you are satisfied that you cannot get a sharp image (wearing distance glasses, where applicable, *not* reading glasses even for the longsighted) you might have to resort to having the eyepiece changed.

With some cameras, this is a simple matter as the manufacturer supplies auxiliary lenses to fit over the existing eyepiece: -2, -3, -4, -5, 0, $+0.5$, $+1$, $+2$, $+3$. The difficulty is in deciding which you want and there is no really satisfactory alternative to trial and error, which is after all, how spectacle lenses are prescribed. You may know your spectacle prescription but you also need to know how the manufacturer quotes his auxiliary lenses. Most of them quote the corrected dioptric power, not the actual power of the lens they supply.

Where the manufacturer does not supply corrective lenses try your optician who should be able to have your eyepiece lens changed by cutting and grinding the lens to your specifications. It might be difficult to find an optician who both understands and is willing to carry out the task, but most people will be able to adjust to the standard eyepieces. It is not generally advisable for spectacle wearers to have their eyepiece lenses changed to allow them to use the camera without their spectacles. With very short-sighted people advancing in age and so having lost their short-range accommodation, it might seem a good idea because they can then use the viewfinder and see the aperture and shutter speed figures on the camera without spectacles. But then they have to put the spectacles back on to view the subject. Better to learn to set the camera controls by touch—as everybody should do, in any case.

Long-sighted people or older people who need spectacles only for reading, must not be deluded into thinking that they should use their reading or close-range spectacles for viewfinding. The eyepiece is adjusted for near normal sight. Although the image is actually close to the eye, the eyepiece lens acts just like a supplementary lens to induce the eye to see the image as if it were much further away. One meter or so is a popular distance, well beyond the range of reading spectacles.
The only case in which there would be a clear-cut argument in favour of a corrected eyepiece is that of eyesight that needs spectacles other than distance spectacles to see objects at about 1–2 m, where most screen images are placed. Some are placed much further out but then normal distance spectacles should give perfectly clear vision or at least the best vision that is possible for that type of eyesight.
The temptation to have an eyepiece adjusted often arises from the damage that eyepiece frames can do to spectacle lenses. Considering the number of people who wear spectacles, camera manufacturers are strangely insensitive to their needs. There are few, if any, cameras that allow a clear view of the whole field to *all* spectacle wearers and many of them have hard-rimmed eyepieces. Rubber eyecups are certainly available but they are designed for the naked eye, as they more or less have to be, considering the size and variety of modern spectacle lenses. The only satisfactory answer is to modify the eyepiece yourself with a foam or rubber surround.

Magnifiers

The viewfinder eyepiece may be quite suitable for general photography but there can be occasions when you need a closer view for fine detail. There is an apparently simple answer to that, but it has one very large snag for most cameras.
Focusing magnifiers are provided by both camera and independent manufacturers. They clip on to the viewfinder eyepiece and provide a magnified (2.5X up to 7X or so) view of the central portion of the viewfinder image. Most of them are well made and easy to use. They generally incorporate an eyesight correction capability

(useful in this case) and are hinged at the top so that they can be rapidly flipped out of the way to allow a view of the whole field after focusing.

Unfortunately, it might not be the centre of the field that you want to magnify. Even if it is, that is the one area in most reflexes on which you cannot focus except by that iniquitous rangefinder spot. So, if you have the now almost universal split-image rangefinder spot surrounded by a microprism collar, the magnifier is virtually useless—and the greater its magnification the more useless it becomes. These magnifiers can, in fact, be used satisfactorily only with plain, fine-ground screens. To provide a brighter, more evenly illuminated image, even some modern screens are not as fine-ground as they might be. The texture of the screen can often break up the finest detail and in those circumstances, too, the magnifier is of little value.

Magnifiers are also available for ordinary screen focusing cameras, of course. In that case, however, they do not need to be attached to the camera. Almost any magnifier will do and you can use it anywhere on the screen.

Angle finders

A more useful eyepiece accessory is the angle finder. There are many occasions in copying, photomicrography, low-level shooting, etc. when it may be inconvenient or even impossible to get an eye to the eyepiece. The angle finder is an L-shaped construction with a mirror box in the angle. Attached to the camera eyepiece, it can be rotated through 360° to allow viewing from a variety of angles.

The mirror necessarily causes the image to be laterally reversed, which can be awkward to those not accustomed to it. Angle finders are commonly used in relatively static set-ups, however, where the wrong-way-round image does not often raise problems. Some models do provide a double-reflected image to correct the lateral reversal but they cost more, and even the standard type is quite expensive. Most models incorporate an eyesight correction control that allows the finder to be used without spectacles by all except the very shortsighted.

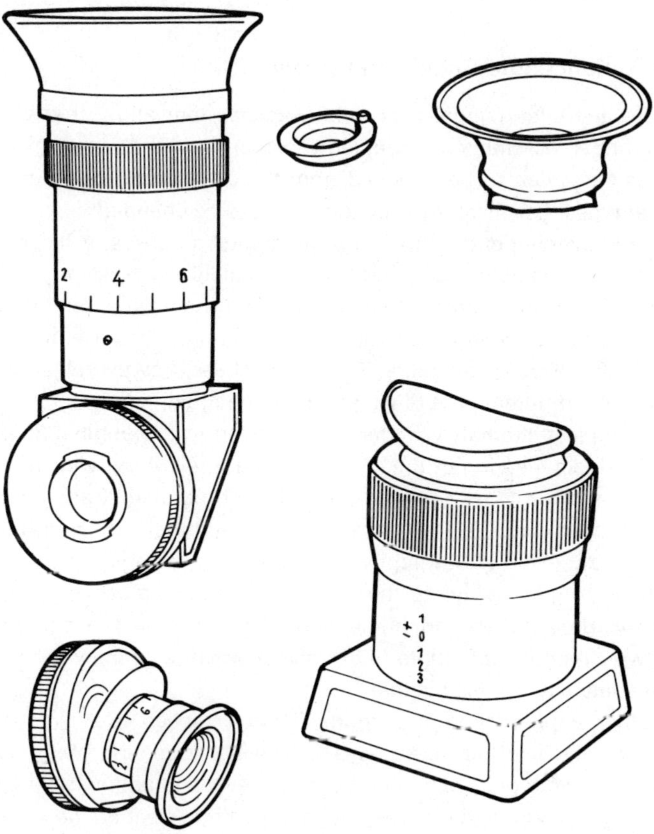

The right-angle finder (*top left*) allows viewing from almost any angle. The soft rubber eyecup (*top right*) sometimes accommodates a correction lens holder. Screen-image magnifiers (*bottom*) may show part or all of the image. The hinge allows the magnifier to be swung out when not required.

There is little standardization in eyepiece construction, so angle finders and, indeed, most other eyepiece attachments, have to be tailored to individual camera models. Some slot into grooves; others require a clamping ring to be removed and replaced; some have even had bayonet attachments. Angle finders are therefore generally available only as equipment for specific cameras. There are one or two independent makes but only for the most popular camera models.

Interchangeable finders and screens

There are a few single-lens-reflex cameras that allow the whole viewfinder assembly of eyepiece, pentaprism and viewing and focusing screen to be removed from the camera and changed for other types. Others allow only the screen to be changed.

The removable pentaprism can have various purposes. It has been used for example, to permit a TTL metering system to be incorporated in a camera that previously did not have one. It can allow automatic exposure facilities to be brought into use or add a low-light-reading capability. The principal use, however, has been to allow a different type of viewfinder to be fitted.

The simplest alternative finder is a reversion to the original 35 mm SLR—direct viewing of the screen instead of eye-level viewing via the pentaprism. A magnifier is generally incorporated. Many people prefer this view in relatively static set-ups and there are occasions, as in low-level photography, when it is preferable. It is very difficult to get any eye to the normal eyepiece of a camera placed on the ground, and an angle finder may not be the complete answer. As with the angle finder, direct waist-level viewing gives you a laterally reversed image.

Another popular type is a sports finder or speed finder, as one maker calls it. That one has a swivelling eyepiece on a more orthodox pentaprism allowing both eye-level and alternative-angle viewing—downward for low-level or upward to clear the heads in a crowd and various other alternatives. It is useful in photomicrography and copying and many other applications because, apart from the choice of angles, it gives a full view of the screen with the eye up to 2.5 inches behind the eyepiece. This is

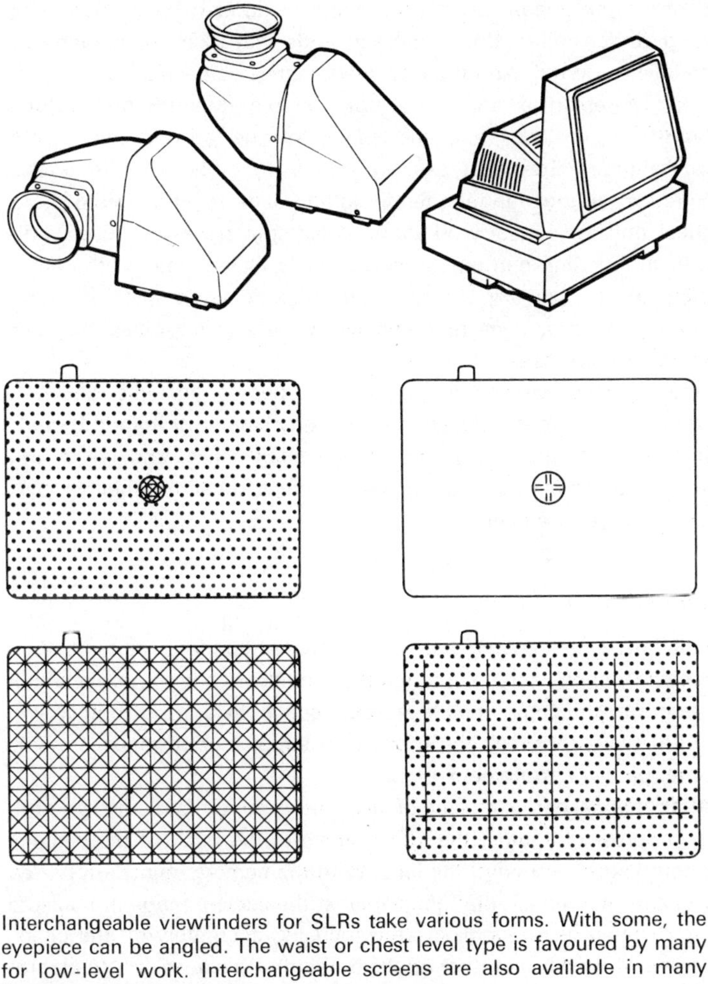

Interchangeable viewfinders for SLRs take various forms. With some, the eyepiece can be angled. The waist or chest level type is favoured by many for low-level work. Interchangeable screens are also available in many forms for specialized work.

especially useful if you use the camera in an underwater housing. Alternative finders are available only for specific cameras and there are no universal or independent brands. They usually also allow the viewing screen to be changed and, in this case, independently manufactured alternatives are available.

The popular standard screen at present is a fine-ground type with a central split-image rangefinder spot surrounded by a microprism rangefinder collar. Not everybody finds that ideal, particularly for specialized work. About a dozen alternative screens are made. The effectiveness of a rangefinder, for example, depends on the focal length of the lens and the angles of the prisms forming the rangefinder. Special types are made for longer-focus lenses. Screens without rangefinder spots are made for those who prefer them and for critical work such as extreme close-ups. Even more critical focusing can be carried out on a plain screen with central crossed lines giving a form of parallax focusing with an aerial image. Lined screens or graticules are useful for measuring and lining-up purposes.

Again, these screens are made for specific cameras but it is possible to have the screen in almost any camera changed. It could be expensive but, if you are going to specialize, and feel happy with your camera except for its screen, it must be cheaper than buying a new cameera.

Checking the focus

Not strictly a viewing aid, but in the same field, perhaps, is a focusing check screen. You might sometimes have a doubt about the mirror or screen line up in your camera. With a non-reflex, you might want to check the focus of a supplementary lens or some other piece of equipment.

All that is needed is a piece of very fine-ground glass small enough to be pressed against the film runners in the back of the camera, ground surface toward the lens. With the camera rigidly supported you can then check the focus against the screen image or measure the distance to the subject after focusing accurately on the check screen. A small magnifier could be helpful because the small size of the image tends to sharpen it. Always carry out the test with the lens set to full aperture, not only for the best illumination but to reduce depth of field as far as possible. Keep the back of the camera shaded, too, to increase contrast.

There is little point in checking the focusing scale engraved on the lens except to confirm that it is drastically adrift and the lens needs attention. It is necessarily compressed and imprecise and you cannot set it accurately.

A commercial version of the focusing check screen is available, with useful hints on its applications.

What You Need for Close-ups

Close-up is an indefinite term in photography. When lenses commonly focused no closer than about 1.5 m while attached to the camera, close-up photography could be any shot taken from less than that distance. For some fixed-lens cameras it might still apply. Generally, however, the standard lens of a 35 mm SLR can focus to 60 cm or less and, although that might be considered close range, it is not generally regarded as close-up photography.

Perhaps there is no better definition than that the term close-up means photography carried out at closer range than the normal focusing mechanism of the camera allows. We have already raised one objection to that and it is also true that many technical and other bellows-focusing cameras can focus close enough even for life-size (1:1) reproduction. It is adequate for most purposes, however, and makes the point that close-up photography generally calls for special accessories. These accessories rely on two methods of enabling the camera to be used closer to the subject.

To focus closer, a camera lens has to be moved further away from the image plane, where the film is located. When the image-lens distance is equivalent to the focal length (actually fractionally more) the focused distance is out at infinity—far, far away. As the lens-to-image distance is increased, the focused distance becomes nearer. Cameras using rigid lenses (no bellows) have a limited amount of movement built into the lens—limited because the closer you get the greater the necessary movement of the lens becomes. To get to 1:1 reproduction, you have to move the lens forward by a distance equivalent to its focal length, while getting down to one meter or so involves only a few millimeters of movement.

The first approach to allowing a lens to focus closer is simple. If you put another converging lens (all camera lenses are necessarily converging) in front of the camera lens you produce a combination of shorter focal length than the camera lens alone. That combined lens is then effectively further forward for a given focused distance than it should be, because its minimum (infinity) extension is the focal length of the camera lens alone. So you can focus closer. Such an additional lens is known as a supplementary or close-up lens.

The second approach is to increase the lens-to-image distance by placing extension rings or tubes or a bellows construction between the lens and the camera body.

Supplementary lenses

The basic principle of a supplementary or close-up lens is relatively easy to understand. When a lens is separated from the image plane by a distance equal to its focal length, it is focused on a very distant subject from which the rays of light reaching the lens are virtually parallel. That is why we said the distance is actually fractionally greater than the focal length: the rays from the subject must diverge, however fractionally. Similarly, when the lens focuses an object one focal length in front of it, the rays emerging from the back of the lens are parallel.

So, if you set a camera lens to its infinity focusing position and place another lens in front of it, the combination will focus an object at a distance from the supplementary lens equivalent to its focal length. The supplementary lens sends parallel rays to the camera lens, which accepts them as coming from infinity and bends them to form an image. The point of all this is that there is no mystique about a supplementary lens. Any lens can be used, always providing that it is a converging (positive) and not diverging (negative) lens. You can even use another camera lens as an extremely strong supplementary. There is no question of compatibility or of one maker's supplementary lenses not being usable on another maker's cameras.

The only occasion when some difficulty can arise is when the supplementary lens maker does not tell you the actual focal length of his lenses and you want to use them on a fixed-lens camera with no focusing screen. You cannot see the image so you have to measure the focused distance. If the lenses were designed for a particular camera and the maker tells you only that they are numbers 1, 2 and 3 and they focus at certain stated distances from the focal plane of his camera, you will have some difficulty.

There is another possibility, too, also concerning non-reflex cameras but this time only the simpler type with fixed-focus lenses. The focus at which such lenses are fixed is rarely stated, but it is certainly not infinity. So you cannot rely on a supplementary lens focusing at its own focal length. You have to use the camera maker's supplementary lenses, if he supplies them, or make rather a lot of experiments.

None of these problems arises with screen-focusing cameras. You see the effect of the supplementary lens on the screen and you focus in the normal way.

Supplementary lenses are generally single glass types of relatively low power, expressed in the optician's term of dioptres. A few manufacturers sensibly quote focal lengths. When they do not, you have to convert the dioptre strength into focal length by dividing the dioptre number into one metre. A 2-dioptre lens has a focal length of 500 mm and focuses an object at that distance in front of it when attached to a camera lens focused at infinity. The only value of the dioptre number in photography is in calculations. Dioptre numbers can be added together to indicate combined strength, whereas the calculation of the combined focal length provided by two lenses is more complex. It is easier to convert the focal lengths to dioptre strengths by dividing them into 1 metre; then add together these figures, and convert them back to focal lengths by again dividing them into 1 metre. For example, a 50 mm lens is 20 dioptres (1000/50) and a 100 mm lens is 10 dioptres (1000/100). Added together they form a 30 dioptre combination which has a focal length of 33 mm (1000/30). Lenses up to about 4 dioptres are relatively inexpensive. Those of greater power need to be of better quality and can become much more expensive. Some are of more than one-glass construction.

Should you buy close-up lenses, or are they inferior substitutes for more sophisticated close-up equipment? If you have a fixed-lens camera you have no alternative. With an interchangeable-lens camera, you do have the alternative of increasing the lens extension, and some will unhesitatingly condemn the supplementary lens in favour of extension tubes and bellows.

As with so many photographic matters, the true facts are not so clear cut. The theory is plain. A supplementary lens is optically imperfect, of course, but you are not using it alone. Any one element from your 14-element camera lens could be said to be imperfect, too. Theory is not enough. In practice, supplementary lenses can give excellent results. The argument that extra extension avoids the use of an optically imperfect product is untenable. Few camera lenses are designed to operate at very short subject distances.

Supplementary lenses have other significant advantages. They are normally supplied in the same form as filters, to screw or bayonet into the front of the lens in no time at all. They have no effect on light transmission and the screen image remains bright and easy to focus. Even with a viewfinder camera, it is not difficult to improvise a focusing jig.

At very close range, you are working with extremely limited depth of field and often beyond the flat-field capability of a wide-aperture camera lens. So you work at small apertures and make no use of the outer areas of the supplementary lens, which might indeed cause poor image quality. Certainly the average supplementary lens does not offer very great magnification, unless you use it on a longer focus lens, and higher power types have to be expensive to be good. At moderate reproduction ratios, it is a completely acceptable close-up device on any type of camera.

To buy a supplementary lens, decide on the approximate reproduction ratio or magnification that you want. We use the term magnification in this sense although, more often than not, we actually mean reduction. Reproduction ratio is expressed in the form 1:2, meaning that one unit of linear measurement on the film represents two units of the subject. In this case, an object 4 cm long would be reproduced as 2 cm long on the film (half life size). Life size is 1:1, twice life size is 2:1 and so on.

Magnification is expressed as a single figure. Life size is 1 (M=1), half life size is 0.5 and twice life size is 2.

The magnification provided by supplementary lenses is proportional to dioptre strength or focal length of both supplementary and camera lens, when the camera lens is set to infinity. A one-dioptre lens gives a 0.05 (one-twentieth life size) magnification with a 50 mm lens or 0.2 with a 200 mm lens. A 4-dioptre gives a 0.2 magnification with a 50 mm lens or 0.4 with a 100 mm, and so on.

Having decided on the magnification you want and the dioptre strength that entails, check the filter attachment of your camera. Most are now screw-fitting in a standard series, commonly running from 49 mm to 58 mm. Order up your lens quoting the dioptre number and the filter thread.

If you have any difficulty in identifying your filter fitting, take your camera to a dealer to make sure that you get a lens that fits. It simply has to attach securely to the camera lens. It does not matter how it is fixed. Some cameras use push-on fittings, others use a sprung ring and a clamp screw.

There is an exception to the dictum that supplementary lenses cannot provide very great magnification. They can if they are of sufficiently good quality. There are a few 10-dioptre types about that can just about make it but that is the limit—unless you use a camera lens. To use this method effectively, however, you need a telephoto lens and a standard lens in your collection—a usual practice. Various combinations can be used but a 135 mm lens on the camera and a 50 mm lens on the front is probably most practicable. Attachment is simple in most cases because manufacturers provide coupling rings to join the two filter threads together. The 50 mm is thus reversed on the 135 mm. This combination is effectively a 20-dioptre supplementary on the 135 mm camera lens and it gives a magnification of 2.7 on the film.

The magnification provided by a supplementary lens on any given camera lens is derived from a quite complicated formula but you can take a short cut by simply dividing the focal length of the supplementary into the focal length of the camera lens. A 50 mm lens on a 200 mm set to infinity gives a magnification of 4.

Special types of close-up lens are also available. Their advantages compared with the normal types are debatable, particularly in view of their considerably higher price. There is a variable type, for example, that changes its focal length rather like a zoom lens, and

allows a greater range of focused distances than is available with an ordinary supplementary lens and the camera lens focusing mechanism.
Another type is part close-up lens and part clear glass, enabling you to focus very close and very distant objects at the same time. The idea is to give the illusion of great depth of field. The illusion is generally obvious because, naturally, the two focused planes have to be in different parts of the picture and the dividing line can rarely be realistically concealed. The area between the two focused planes (or part of it at least) is inevitably out of focus and that is even more difficult to cope with.

Extension tubes

Supplementary lenses can give very good results at moderate reproduction ratios. A 4-dioptre lens, for example, on a 50 mm camera lens set to infinity, can give a ratio of only about 1:5. Even a 10-dioptre lens in such circumstances can only reach 1:2. You can increase these ratios proportionately by using longer-focus camera lenses but it *is* generally preferable when working at reproduction ratio greater than about 1:5 to use the alternative method. Increased dioptre strength brings the risk of inferior quality except at unrealistic cost.
Extension tubes need not be expensive. Some camera manufacturers' types are offered at exceptionally high prices that cannot really be justified, so it pays to shop around among the independent brands. If you have a complicated camera linkage, however, some of these independent brands may not operate satisfactorily in all the automatic functions. In most cases that is not important because the set-up is often relatively static and you are not unduly rushed. You may prefer full performance, however, when using a single short tube simply to enable you to focus a little closer with a long-focus lens.
Generally speaking, extension tubes are suitable only for single-lens reflexes or other screen focusing cameras. On such cameras, their length, construction, etc. is relatively unimportant. You can improvise with cardboard or plastic tubes if you blacken the inside. The screen shows the effect precisely. Naturally, you lose any

auto-diaphragm or other special links but it is no great hardship to use the diaphragm manually or operate the meter in the stopped-down mode.

When tubes are used on interchangeable-lens cameras without focusing screen facilities, their exact length and effect on focused distance must be known. Such information is rarely available these days. When these cameras were more popular, various focusing aids were available, from a simple screen box that temporarily replaced the camera body to a full reflex attachment still provided for the Leica.

Extension tubes are normally supplied in a set of three different lengths adding up to about 50 mm. They can be used singly or in any combination to give reproduction ratios up to about 1:1 with a 50 mm lens. Doubling the lens extension gives 1:1 ratio: if you use the 50 mm set on a 100 mm lens, you get only a 1:2 ratio. Theoretically, there is no limit to the number or length of tubes you can put on the camera but the greater the length the lower the illumination at the film plane and the greater the difficulty in focusing. You can, of course, use a powerful lamp for focusing purposes only, or even for the actual photography if your subject will stand it—but it is more likely that at great magnifications you would use electronic flash. You should not use too much tube extension together with an automatic diaphragm facility. That can impose quite a strain on the mechanism. If you must use a lot of tubes, make them the manual type and operate the diaphragm manually—but preferably use a bellows.

Extension bellows

The disadvantage of extension tubes is that each tube allows only a very narrow range of focused distances, using the focusing mechanism of the lens. To change the reproduction ratio significantly you have to remove the lens and change the tube length. A more flexible arrangement is to use an extension bellows. The basic bellows unit consists of a front and a rear standard attached to a rail or rails and joined by a concertina-like construction of light-proofed material. The front standard carries a lens mount and can be moved along the rails either manually or by

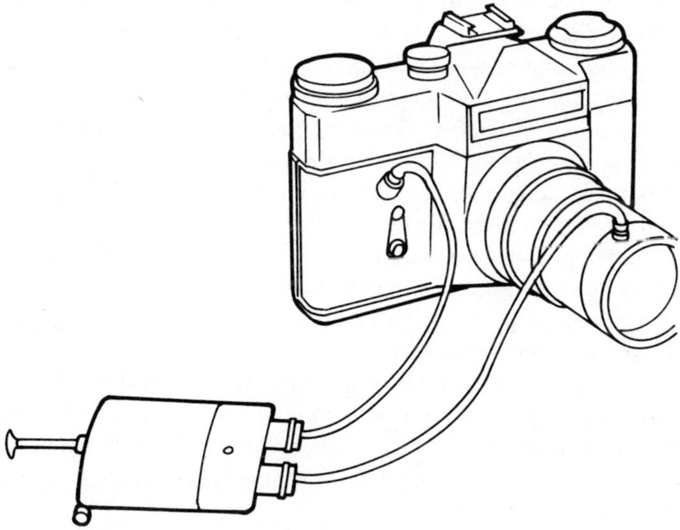

A double cable release and special intermediate ring allow auto-iris operation to be maintained when a lens is reversed or is separated from the camera body by non-automatic accessories.

a rack and pinion drive. The rear standard carries a camera mount and is often fixed to the rails but is movable in some models. Locking knobs are provided to hold the bellows at any required extension.

The thickness of the standards imposes a minimum extension, generally in the region of 20-30 mm for 35 mm cameras. Maximum extension depends on the length of the bellows and varies with design and price. It is not often greater than 200 mm. There is an obvious conflict here between rigidity and size.

A notable point with bellows is that none of them provides all the trouble-free links with camera controls that can be made available on well-constructed tubes. The bellows makes a direct link impossible so various indirect methods have been devised. Most so-called auto-bellows in fact use double cable releases, one to operate the camera shutter and the other the lens diaphragm.

The disadvantage is not always as great as it might seem. A bellows set-up is customarily static and you normally have plenty of time to take meter readings, adjust the lighting, set the camera controls and so on. In fact, it can be said with considerable justification that some manufacturers waste both time and money struggling to provide semi-automatic facilities. The product becomes very expensive, while it should be possible to make a sturdy, uncomplicated bellows at a reasonable price.

All bellows units are provided with a tripod socket in the rear standard and they should have one in the front standard, too, for the occasions when you want to use them with heavy lenses. The camera mount on the rear standard should also allow the camera to be turned to give vertical or horizontal views, preferably with click stops in those positions.

When you decide to buy a bellows unit, you will find that some are shockingly expensive. Some camera manufacturers and independents appear to think there is no demand for a straightforward gimmick-free bellows, being, presumably, deterred by the low profit margin.

There are some simple independent products but they tend to be rather flimsy. Probably the only really stout unit at a reasonable price is the small bellows in the Praktica range of accessories but that has the M42 thread system.

You must examine the bellows unit of your choice before buying, if at all possible. You might need it for a long time and it is essential that it is of absolutely rigid construction. The standards must not be capable of even fractional movement in any direction once locked. The stouter the rail or rails the better. Don't deride one-rail units. They can come up to standard if properly made. Rack-and-pinion drive is useful but by no means essential. Extension, magnification, exposure-adjustment and similar markings are totally unnecessary and are even misleading on some models. You must know how to handle all these factors yourself when practising close-range photography. Similarly, automatic-diaphragm and other such mechanisms are of no great value. Exposure metering for close-ups is best carried out with a separate meter if you are not using flash, together with careful calculation of the effect of the extension, the nature of the subject and the lighting.

Bellows extras

Focusing is often difficult at very close range, especially if you want a specific image size known to be provided by a certain bellows extension. The easiest method of focusing then is to set the required extension and move the whole outfit back and forth (or, if more practical, move the subject) until correct focus is achieved.

With the camera on a tripod, that may be less simple. It can be made relatively easy, however, by mounting the bellows on a focusing rail or slide. This holds the bellows rigidly on an additional sliding support, again operated by push-pull or rack-and-pinion drive. Some bellows units incorporate such a slide, or merely a small block (at a price) or have one available as an optional extra. Independent manufacturers' items are also available and can take most other bellows units because the method of attachment is by tripod screw. Again, look for stout construction and positive locks.

It is common practice to reverse the camera lens on a bellows unit because it often gives better results that way. The snag with some M42 screw lenses is that they have no auto/manual switch. When you turn the lens round, you have no means of stopping it down manually except by holding the depth of field button, if any. That could cause significant camera shake. To solve that problem there is a 'reverse pin depresser' that screws on to the rear of the lens and presses the pin into the stopped down position. The other end has a 49 mm female thread to take lens hood or filters.

The same trouble can arise even with the lens the right way round, but some bellows incorporate a pin depresser in the lens mount. Where they do not, or even where they do, a so-called Z-ring can be used. This has a cable-release-operated pin depresser similar to that in extension tubes so that, with a double cable release, a sort of automatic-iris facility is maintained. Naturally, you can also use the Z-ring with the lens reversed.

Reversing the lens

Reversing the lens on the bellows is often accomplished by removing the front standard, turning it round and replacing it, and then clipping the bellows over the front of the lens. On bellows where that is not possible, the lens has to be reversed by means of a reversing ring, which screws into the lens filter thread and has a male thread or bayonet attachment to fit the bellows lens mount.

Copying equipment

Some close-up equipment is specifically designed for copying flat originals and is therefore operated in the vertical mode. It is easier to lay the original flat than to pin it to a vertical surface. The simplest equipment of this type is a stand consisting of four legs, sometimes telescopic, fitted to a ring to which the camera is fastened by its filter thread and through which it photographs the subject.

This type of stand originated with non-reflex cameras and the length of the legs was designed to fix the focused distance for specific lenses and extension tubes. The ends of the legs also indicated the area covered. It is a more versatile instrument than it appears at first sight because its light weight allows it to be carried and used in any location, and not only in the vertical mode.

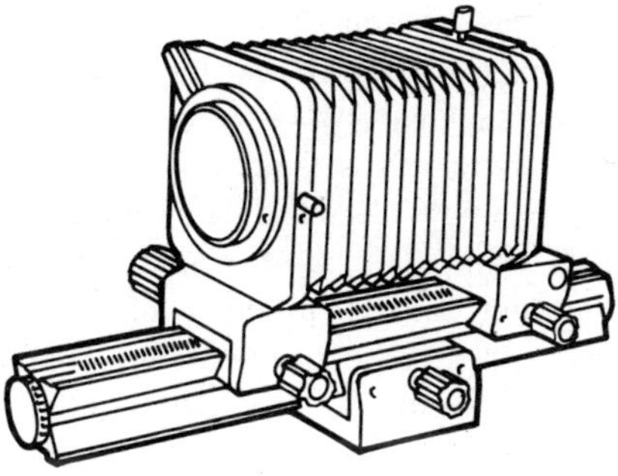

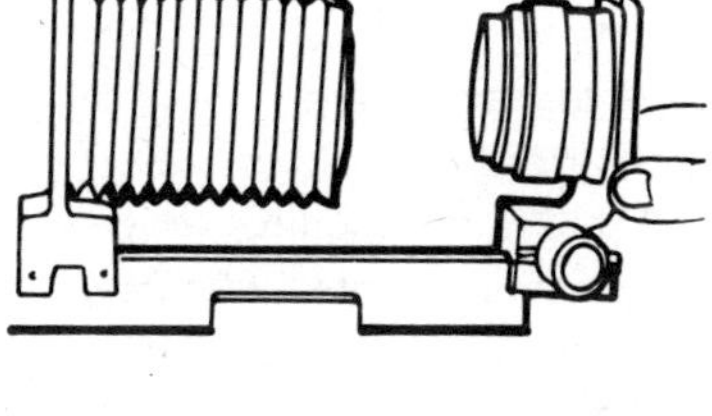

A typical bellows unit incorporating movement of both standards and a focusing slide to allow camera, bellows and lens to be moved as a unit. On many bellows, the lens can be reversed by removing the front standard and replacing it the other way round.

The true copy stand is a much more substantial piece of equipment. It is designed on the same principle as a vertical enlarger and, indeed, many enlargers can easily be converted to copying stands. The basic arrangement is a stout baseboard with a vertical column at the centre of the back edge. Riding up and down the column is a lockable arm to which the camera, bellows unit, focusing slide, etc. are fastened by the tripod screw. For greater security a camera cradle is used with some models. Alternatively a bracket may attach to the arm and provide a means of attaching the camera by its lens filter thread. Either arrangement generally aims to centre the lens over the baseboard.

Lighting set-ups are available to fit most copy stands. They normally take the form of lampholders and reflectors on flexible, swan-neck arms with fittings for standard ES lamps. Two lamps may attach to the stand column or four may be provided to clip near the corners of the baseboard.

Copying stands can be expensive and they occupy rather a lot of space. Many enlargers may, however, be converted to copying stands merely by removing the lamphouse and attaching a repro arm or copying attachment. This is a very simple bracket (that can cost an incredibly high price) with tripod screw fitting to take camera, bellows unit, etc. Lighting equipment may also be available to attach to the bracket. If you are thinking of buying an enlarger and also expect to need a copying stand, this is a point worth considering. Prices of the attachments and lighting units vary considerably.

Slide duplicating

Colour reversal, slide or transparency film—call it what you will—has one big disadvantage. The final picture appears on the film you put in the camera. There is no negative from which you can make further copies. You can make prints, of course, or have them made, but that is not quite the same thing. If you want more than one slide of the same subject you have to shoot it the required number of times or copy the original. The first alternative is obviously impractical in most cases so various types of slide duplicator or copier have become available.

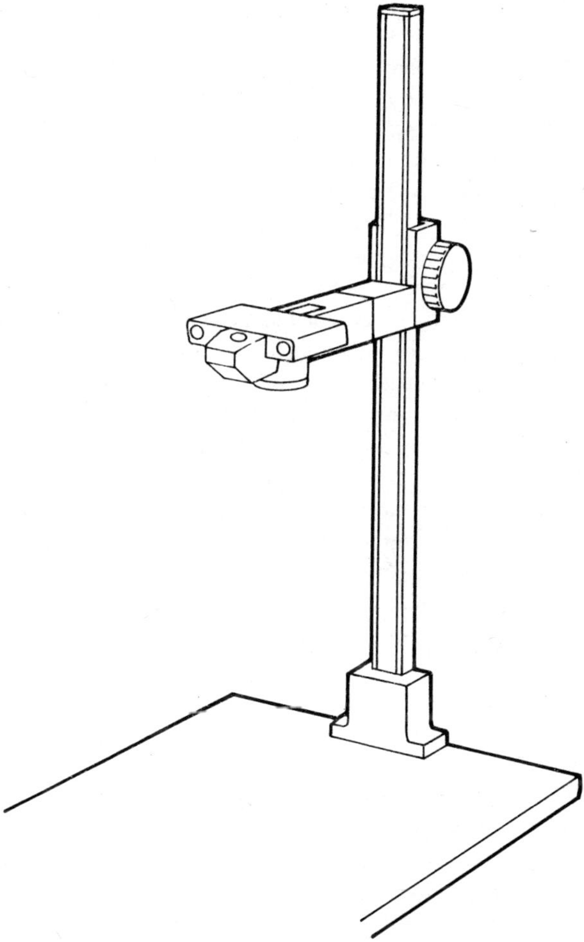

A copying stand is often no more than an enlarger with the head removed and a camera holder attached in its place. Lighting units are available to clamp to the edge of the baseboard.

Copying a slide is simply another form of normal copying and it can be carried out with ordinary close-up equipment. The illumination has to come from behind the slide and must be perfectly even, but that is not difficult to arrange. You could simply fasten the slide over a suitably sized opening in a large black-painted board. Put a piece of white translucent plastic material or opal glass, behind it, and shoot it with your camera set up on a tripod in front with a long sync lead to a small flashgun behind the board. It can be done but it does need a great deal of care in lining up. If you are prepared to spend money, there are easier ways.

If you can afford to, you can buy an elaborate piece of equipment designed to do the job perfectly with just about every control possible. On the lines of a copy stand but a great deal more sophisticated, this type of copier has a substantial base of some depth that houses an adjustable flash unit on rails, a focusing lamp and a lot of wiring. Indicator switches and a meter face you on the top, while behind them, in the horizontal plane, is the copying area proper. This consists of an aperture through which the slide is illuminated, a diffuser plate, filter drawer and interchangeable slide holder. An attachment allows a separate, low-power flashgun to bounce light off a mirror to control contrast by fogging. Rising behind the aperture is a twin-rail assembly carrying a bellows unit to take any type of camera and lens.

Most of us have to manage with less than that and, indeed, would need to be consuming film at a vast rate to pay for it. Fortunately, simpler equipment is available. Perhaps the simplest for those who already possess extension bellows is the slide copier attachment designed for that bellows.

Bellows-attaching duplicators are of more or less standard design, the construction varying somewhat with price. They attach to the front of the bellows rail and consist of a small bellows with lens clamping ring on the front standard. There is no rail: the bellows is simply pulled out and attached to the front of the camera lens (on the main bellows).

The rear standard of the copier bellows has an aperture or film gate, a slot into which slides or film strips can be inserted and a diffuser screen through which the illumination is directed. Electronic flash is the most popular light source. Daylight can be

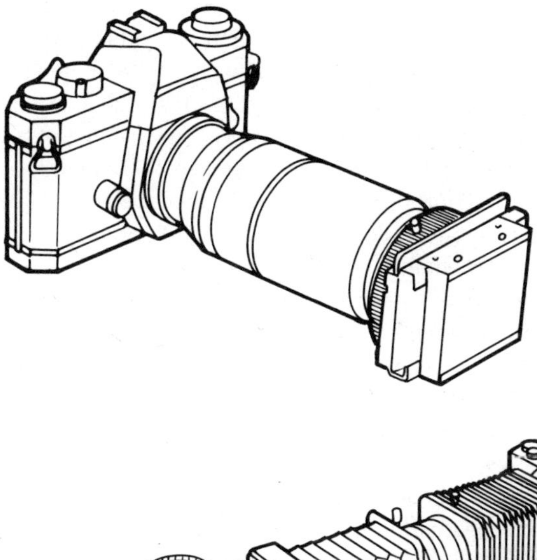

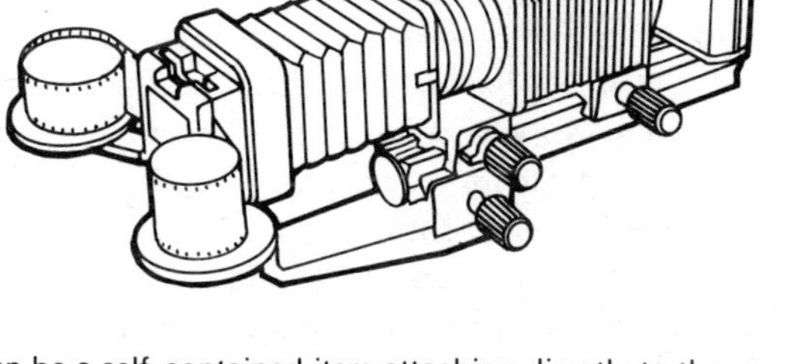

A slide copier can be a self-contained item attaching directly to the camera body. It has its own lens working at a fixed small aperture. Alternatively, the camera's own lens and bellows can be used in conjunction with a slide-holder and auxiliary bellows.

used but is naturally less reliable in both intensity and colour quality. Some duplicators of this type allow a limited amount of movement of the slide so that selective enlargements can be made. They should preferably be used with lenses designed for close-range work because they rarely allow the lens to be reversed.

For those who have no bellows or whose bellows unit does not have a slide copier attachment, there are various types of rigid copier. A popular model has its own specially-designed zoom copying lens working at *f*16. Mounted in front of it is a unit containing the normal diffusing screen and film holder plus a filter compartment. The film or slide can be moved into a variety of positions to allow selective enlargements from any part down to one-quarter of the original image area—even off-centre parts. That model is relatively expensive but it does have the advantage of a lens computed for the job, whereas the bellows-attaching copier requires you to use your own lens, which will quite likely not be up to the job. A modified version has a fixed-focal-length lens allowing same-size copies only at a significant reduction in price. Both versions attach directly to the camera via a T-mount adaptor.

Even greater enlargements can be made with this type of duplicator by fitting a tele-extender on the back, allowing the zoom version, for example, to give 4X enlargements. Even at *f*16, however, you need a lot of light for framing. With the zoom out and a tele-extender added, you are effectively at *f*64 and framing can be difficult. You can fold the diffuser down to admit more light and it can also help to hold a magnifying glass or old condenser lens over the slide holder if you have such an item handy. Remember to replace the diffuser before shooting.

At the lower end of the price scale is another rigid version without lens or built-in extension. It attaches to the filter thread of your lens on your own bellows or tubes. Reproduction ratio varies with the lens and extension, while quality depends entirely on the close-up performance of your lens.

The choice of a slide-copying arrangement therefore depends on various matters. For most users, we can rule out the top model designed for mass production. That undoubtedly is the most versatile and will give absolutely first-class copies if properly used. It does depend, of course, on the quality of your own lens and it would be foolish to use it with any lens other than one that has been tested and proved to give the required quality at close range. The same proviso applies to the other copiers without built-in lenses. If your lens cannot give sharp-all-over results right-way-round, it is useless to buy a copier without its own lens, unless it allows the lens to be reversed and your lens can perform adequately in that position. Don't assume that your very expensive camera lens must give good close-up performance. Some of the most complex are the poorest in this area, whereas a quite inexpensive lens of simple construction may be perfect for the job. Try your enlarger lens. That is designed to work at close range and you should have no difficulty in having an adapter made to allow it to be fixed to your camera or bellows for close-range work. In some cases, stock adaptors are readily available.

In deciding whether you really need a slide copier, remember that they can do various other jobs as well. You can improve an existing transparency by copying it through a filter, or you can try various effects with filters or screens, or by combining two transparencies. They are also useful for making negatives from transparencies (and vice-versa with suitable films). This is the only simple way of getting good black-and-white prints from transparencies.

Microscope adapters

Even the most elaborate close-up equipment is not always enough. There is a practical limit to how far you can extend the camera lens from the film plane before running into illumination difficulties. For really massive enlargements of tiny detail, you need special lenses and what better than the lenses designed for that purpose—microscope objectives.

Many camera manufacturers include microscope adapters in their equipment range. They are all of broadly similar construction, allowing the microscope and camera to be rigidly joined together. The construction generally includes an inner tube that attaches to the microscope drawtube with a removable light shield tube that is used when you photograph without the microscope eyepiece. An outer tube is clamped to the inner tube and attached to the camera lens mount in the normal way. An additional clamp is provided where the microscope has non-focusing stages. A screen focusing or reflex camera is, of course, essential.

Most modern microscopes are suitable for photomicrography although the less expensive versions may not have very good eyepieces. In that case, either photograph without the eyepiece at rather lower magnification or change the eyepiece for one more suitable for photography.

The magnification given by a microscope adapter depends on the camera extension (film plane to eyepiece plane) provided by the adapter. It is the visual magnification × camera extension (cm) ÷ 25. Thus, if the adapter gives a 12.5 cm extension, magnification on the film is half the visual magnification of the microscope.

Rigidity of the assembled unit is of the utmost importance in a microscope adapter. Once the various units are fitted together and clamped, they must be incapable of independent movement.

Macro lenses

The difficulty of computing a camera lens to provide satisfactory image quality both at normal shooting distances and at extremely close range inevitably means that many lenses are not really suitable for close-up photography. Just as inevitably this led to the introduction of so-called macro lenses.

A macro lens, as the term is now generally used, is a lens designed to give sharp, flat-field images at close range and also to work well as a normal camera lens. Consequently it has a continuous focusing range much longer than normal. This kind of performance is virtually impossible with large aperture lenses and macro lenses generally have modest maximum apertures of about *f*3.5 or *f*4. The extra focusing travel allows it to focus from infinity down to about 1:2 reproduction ratio (half life size). Most models also have an extension tube to allow 1:1 reproduction.

Thus, the macro lens, usually of standard or twice the standard focal length, is a lens that can be used both for all general photography out to infinity, and for images up to about half life size simply by turning the focusing ring. It is a useful facility but it is a little expensive and, if you get one in place of your standard lens, it will leave you with a modest maximum aperture. It is also rather bulkier than the standard lens.

The macro tag has spread to other lenses and there are many long-focus and zoom lenses that have a similar capability—but only by operating a separate control to bring the macro mode into operation. These lenses work normally with the macro control inoperative and give images up to about one-third life size in the macro mode. It is a useful facility, particularly with short zooms, which may not otherwise focus very close. There is a 39–80 mm zoom, for example, that focuses no closer than 2 m in normal operation but can get down to 25 cm from the film plane in the macro mode.

In this context, of course, the term 'macro' is a total misnomer. Macro, if it is to mean anything at all in photography, must mean more than life size on the film. None of the popular, so-called macro lenses can do that unaided. Most of these macro-focusing camera lenses require reversing when used at magnifications much greater than 1.

There are one or two genuine macro lenses produced for camera systems but they are generally based on microscope objectives. They are very small, have no focusing mechanisms and are used in conjunction with bellows units and copy stands. They are generally designed to work at 4 or 5X magnification and greater, and are extremely expensive.

Bellows lenses

A number of the longer-focus macro-focusing designs are available in short-mount versions with no focusing mechanism. These go on bellows units to provide a continuous focusing range from infinity down to a reproduction ratio of greater than life size. On the few bellows that give the automatic diaphragm operation, these lenses are excellent for outdoor work, providing a versatile and light, though bulky, outfit.

A few manufacturers offer these lenses with a separate focusing mount, so that you can use them as normal 'Macro' lenses as well. The focusing mount itself acts as a variable length extension tube—providing a compromise between tubes and bellows. Some similar focusing tubes are also available without a matching short-mount lens.

Making the Most of Flash

Flashbulbs are still available but, except in the smallest sizes for some cartridge-loading and instant-picture cameras, they have fallen out of popular use. Even where they are still used, they are generally in cubes or other special constructions.

A flashbulb is a filled glass bulb that burns out with one use. Most types are fired from batteries but there are one or two that are fired by a trip mechanism in the camera which produces a piezo-electric spark. Magicubes do not use electrical firing at all. The camera trips a spring-loaded arm in the cube which strikes a blob of firing paste and thus ignites the bulb.

Bulbs are sold singly or in various proprietary packs that attach to specific cameras and fire each bulb in sequence. The first of these was the flash cube, containing four small bulbs, each with its own reflector. You can use this type of flash in a suitable holder with any flash-synchronized camera. Its main use, though, is as a directly-mounted light source on cameras with a suitable socket. On most cameras the cube rotates with the film advance to bring a fresh bulb into position. On the simplest, though, and if you use a separate flashcube holder, you have to rotate the cube manually. The Magicube looks like a flashcube but requires an entirely different socket, and cannot be used on a separate holder. It can, however, be used with an extender which moves the cube flash further from the lens axis, thus reducing the chance of producing red-eyed portraits. Other types may carry more bulbs in a vertical arrangement that remains fixed but fires each bulb in turn. Each of these units needs its own attachment and firing method built in to the camera.

Of the single bulbs, the AG3 type is the most popular—a small bulb fitting into a flashgun consisting of a case containing a battery, capacitor and resistor, with a reflector, often a folding type attached. The bulb flashgun can be extremely small and light and yet take bulbs giving a remarkably powerful light—much more powerful than a lot of small electronic flash units. There are now comparatively few of them on the market.

The flashbulb, in whatever form, still makes a lot of sense for the occasional user and very powerful types are still available. Nevertheless, they are rarely used these days. The appeal of an electronic flash tube that fires over and over again and so eliminates the need to carry a supply of bulbs has proved irresistible. Further development to provide automatic exposure control and links with the camera's exposure meter have made flashbulbs look old-fashioned.

Electronic flash principles

Electronic flash is provided by an electrical discharge across a gap between two wires (electrodes) in a gas-filled tube. The gas content is adjusted to provide a light close to the colour quality of daylight. The firing circuit is much more complicated than that of a bulb flashgun and, for equivalent power, a great deal more expensive. There are many small and inexpensive electronic flash units but they are generally very low-powered.

The tube can vary in size from tiny to huge with consequent variations in power, circuitry, size of components and price. There is, literally, something for everybody, from the tiny unit smaller than a cigarette pack to studio consoles with power units that have to move about on wheels. The working life of the tube is measured in seconds but, as the duration of each flash is in the region of 1/1000 second or less, the average user rarely wears out a tube.

The great advantages of flash, for professionals at least, are its predictability, ease of handling and lack of heat on the subject. Many studios are geared to more or less standard flash set-ups that can be modified at will to suit particular applications. The large lamp units take a variety of forms to give flood or spot lighting and can be fitted with accessories to shade, concentrate or otherwise modify the effect. Modelling lamps of relatively low power are generally built in to allow the effect to be gauged before the flash units are brought into operation.

Similar advantages are available to the amateur or hobby photographer on a smaller scale. His units do not have as many accessories but they have far greater portability and manoeuvrability. They are convenient in use and, again, do not require him to overheat his subject under the glare of powerful incandescent lamps. The smaller units, too, like small-format cameras, tend to make greater use of electronics to provide automatic-exposure facilities.

Automatic exposure is provided by high-speed electronic switching. A sensor in the flash unit body measures the light reflected from the subject and cuts off the power to the tube when sufficient light has been emitted to give correct exposure. At very close range that can lead to exposures shorter than 1/50,000 second and a consequent increase in the number of flashes per tube or set of batteries.

For complete portability, battery power is essential, but most units can also be operated from the home power supply via a small transformer/rectifier package. These are quite inexpensive but are generally designed for use on specific units. They plug directly into a power supply with a lead to the flash unit that also cuts off the manual switch. Batteries can be awkward because the average number of flashes per set of batteries is in the region of 50 or so, with a marked increase in recycling time (the time needed to recharge the capacitors) after about 20 or so flashes. Batteries with greater capacity are available but at a significant increase in cost. Rechargeable batteries are also costly, and when they are built in to a flash gun, they can be very limiting. Once you have used up the charge you have to do without the flash, usually for several hours, while you recharge it.

Choosing an electronic flash unit

There is a wide variety of electronic flash units available and your choice, as always, should depend on the amount of use to which you expect to put the unit and the type of work you intend doing. The more ambitious you are, or the more you prefer automation to calculation, the more you have to pay.

The cheapest units are small and low-powered to the point of uselessness. Nevertheless, if your only intended use is in very close-range shots or as fill-in daylight, even one of these units can have its use.

You judge the power of the unit from its guide number. Practically all units short of the large studio types are given a guide number rather than a figure denoting electrical output, which can be rather misleading. The guide number is arrived at by multiplying together the *f*-number and distance (in feet or meters—two different guide numbers) that give correct exposure for a film of given sensitivity (or speed). The operation of the inverse square law in relation to light sources ensures that any such pair of figures will give the same product.

Thus, a unit with a guide number of 18 (meters) will give correct exposure if the lens is set to *f*8 and the unit is placed a little over two meters from the subject (or *f*4 and 4.5 m, etc.) The really inexpensive units have guide numbers from about 6 or 8 to 24 for 100ASA film. A unit that has a guide number that seems a bit high for its price should be viewed with some suspicion.

On some flash units the guide number is indicated by a table printed on the case or by an exposure dial. The table quotes the actual guide numbers for a few popular film speeds. The dial indicates the guide numbers indirectly. You set the dial to the film speed required and in so doing cause an aperture scale to move against a distance scale. Read off any pair of aperture and distance and multiply them together. That is the guide number for the film speed set. A certain amount of rounding off is usually involved.

Such a dial allows you to check the guide number for any film speed on the scale. Without it, you have to do a little bit of calculation. The guide numbers advance like aperture numbers. Twice the light means a guide number multiplied by the square root of two. Ten times the light means a guide number multiplied by the square root of 10. So, if you have a guide number for 25ASA and you want to know what it should be for 250ASA, you simply multiply by the square root of 10 or 3.16.

In that case, the light is not 10X more powerful, it is 10X more effective, because of the increase in film speed. If you were comparing two flashguns, however, one with a guide number of 20 and the other with a guide number of 63, you would know that the latter was not 3 times more powerful but 3.16 × 3.16, or 10X.

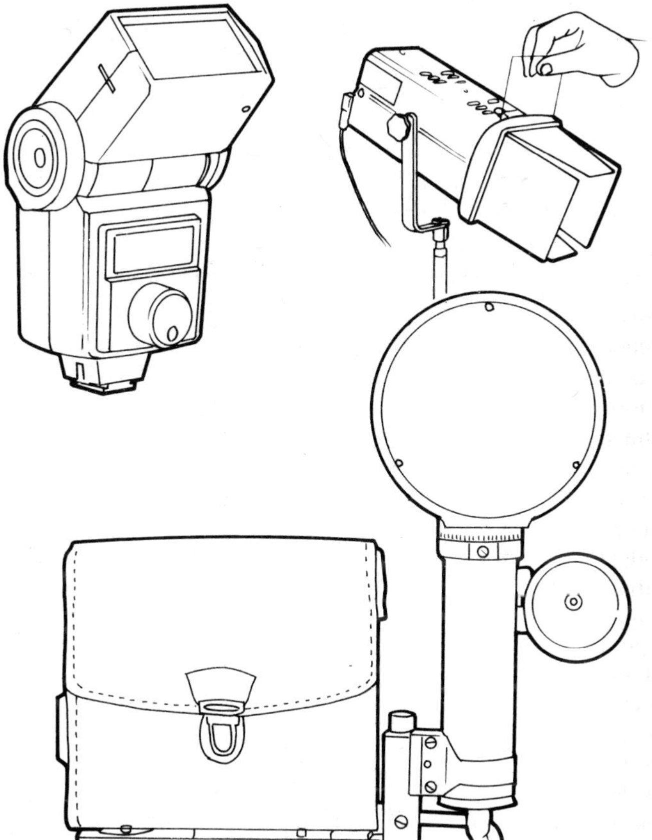

The 'amateur' type electronic flash unit contrasted with a studio type spot with barn doors and filter slot and a sophisticated heavy-duty, high-power type for mobile use.

But you must make sure you are comparing like with like. The guide numbers must relate to the same film speed and must be on the same basis—feet or meters.

For reasonable power, you need a guide number of about 30 upward. At 30 you have power roughly equivalent to that of the smallest flashbulb. At that level, however, the price is no longer low and can be very high indeed. When you are judging power, do not pay too much attention to the often-quoted advantage of being able to stop down to increase depth of field. For that you need quite significantly higher power to increase the shooting distance, because the biggest drawback to flash work (and any other form of artificial illumination) is that its power falls off drastically with distance.

You may be told, for example, that a guide number of 44 allows you to shoot from 4 m at *f*11. So it does, but the small stop gives you limited extra depth of field. With a 50 mm lens, depth of field at those settings stretches from about 2 to 7.5 m. With your main subject correctly lit, however, the object at 2 m would be 4X overexposed and that at 7.5 m nearly 4X underexposed. The small stop gives you extra depth of field but, with one flash unit, you cannot light it adequately.

Extra power is always useful but its value is in allowing you to shoot at reasonable distances (for full-length figures, perhaps) or to use films of moderate speed. You can always reduce the power at close range by using diffusers, filters or an automatic-exposure model but you cannot increase it. You need reasonable power, too, if the unit has accessories such as wide-angle attachments and filters, which can decrease its effective power dramatically.

Apart from power, you have to consider whether you need an automatic-exposure model. Soon, you may not have the choice. Most of the medium-to-high power units are of this type. Those of very low or very high power are often manually-controlled only.

The automatic versions are useful, particularly for those who find any kind of mathematical calculation difficult. You simply set a lens aperture and a switch on the unit in sympathy and shoot, regardless. Provided you are no further from, or nearer to, the subject than the power of the unit can cope with (the limits are shown on the unit) you get adequately exposed pictures. Many

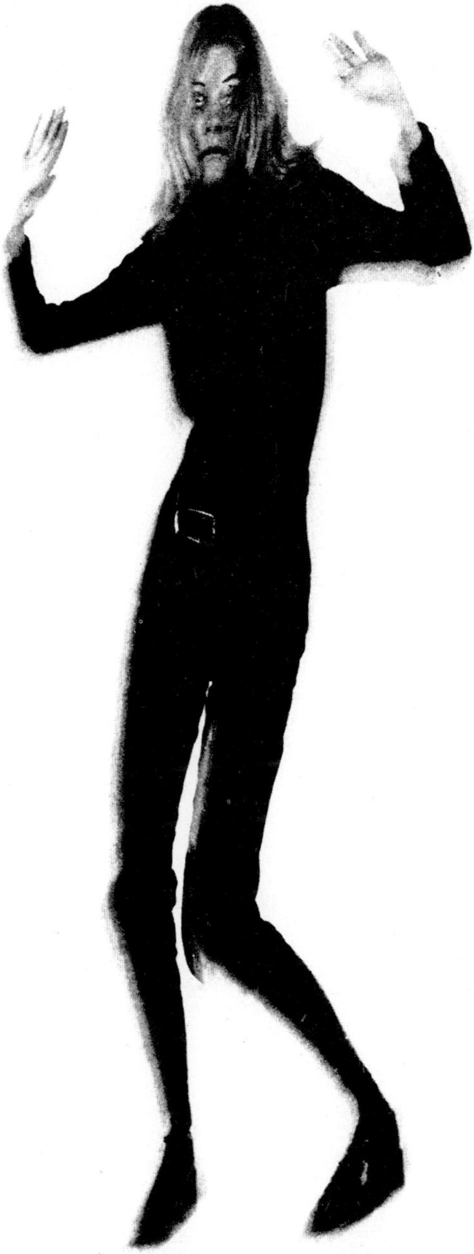

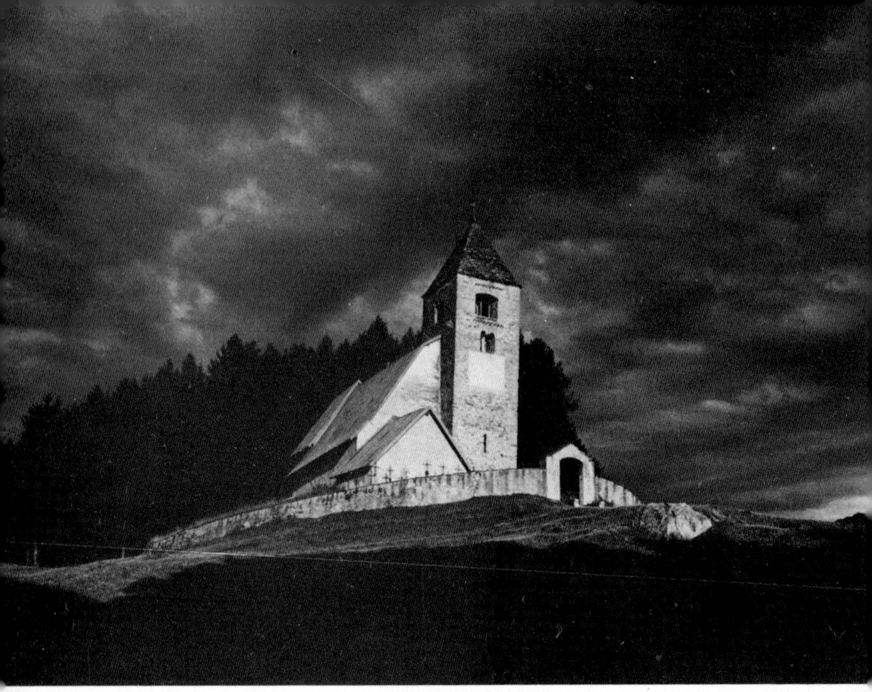

Above Daylight photograph taken on panchromatic film through a deep red filter. *Geri Della Rocca de Candal*

Opposite, top Shows an object photographed at the minimum focusing distance of the lens.

Opposite, bottom Fitting an extension tube between the camera and lens reduces the minimum camera-to-subject distance, enabling small objects to be approached closer to fill the picture frame, and for the photographer to make greater use of differential focus effects. *Hasselblad photograph*

Previous page Distortion effect created by fitting an anamorphic attachment to the front of the camera's lens and rotating it 90° during a $\frac{1}{2}$ second exposure. *Günter Spitzing, Focalguide to Effects and Tricks*

Overleaf Highlight reflections take on a star-shape when photographed through a card or something similar having a suitably shaped cut-out in the centre. *Sidney Ray*

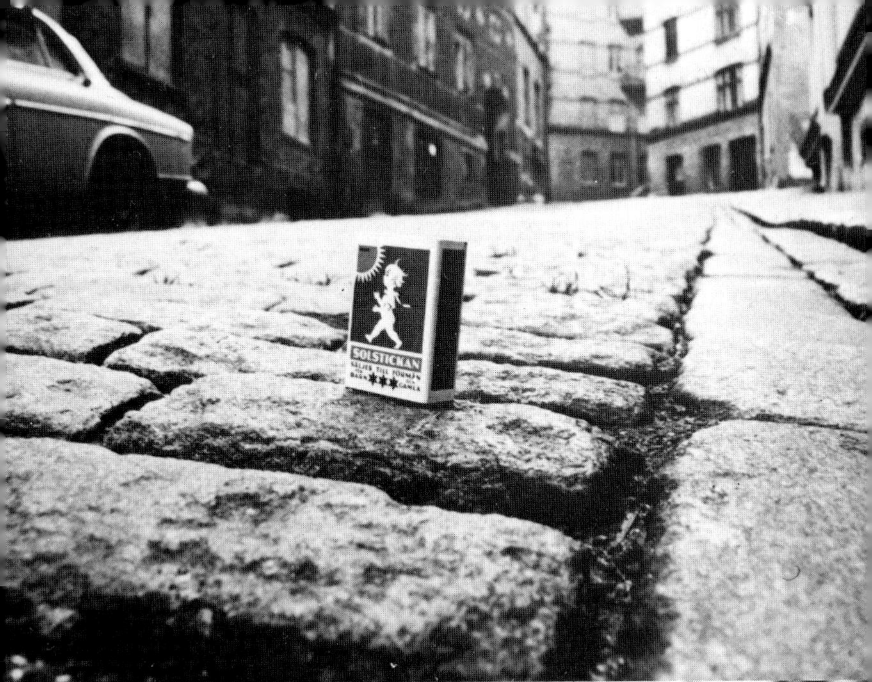
SOLSTICKAN

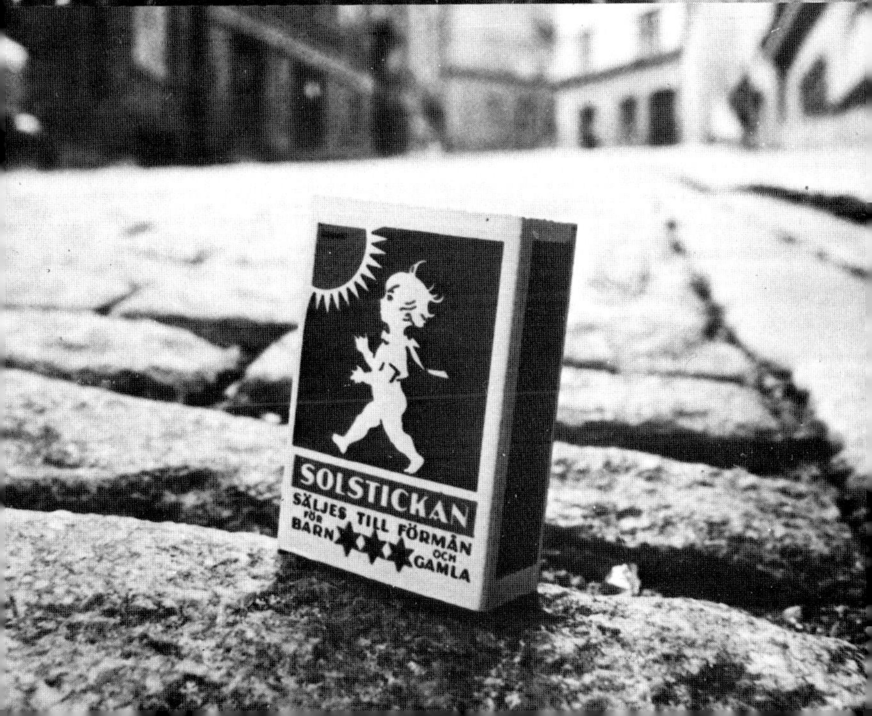
SOLSTICKAN
SÄLJES TILL FÖRMÅN
FÖR
BARN
OCH
GAMLA

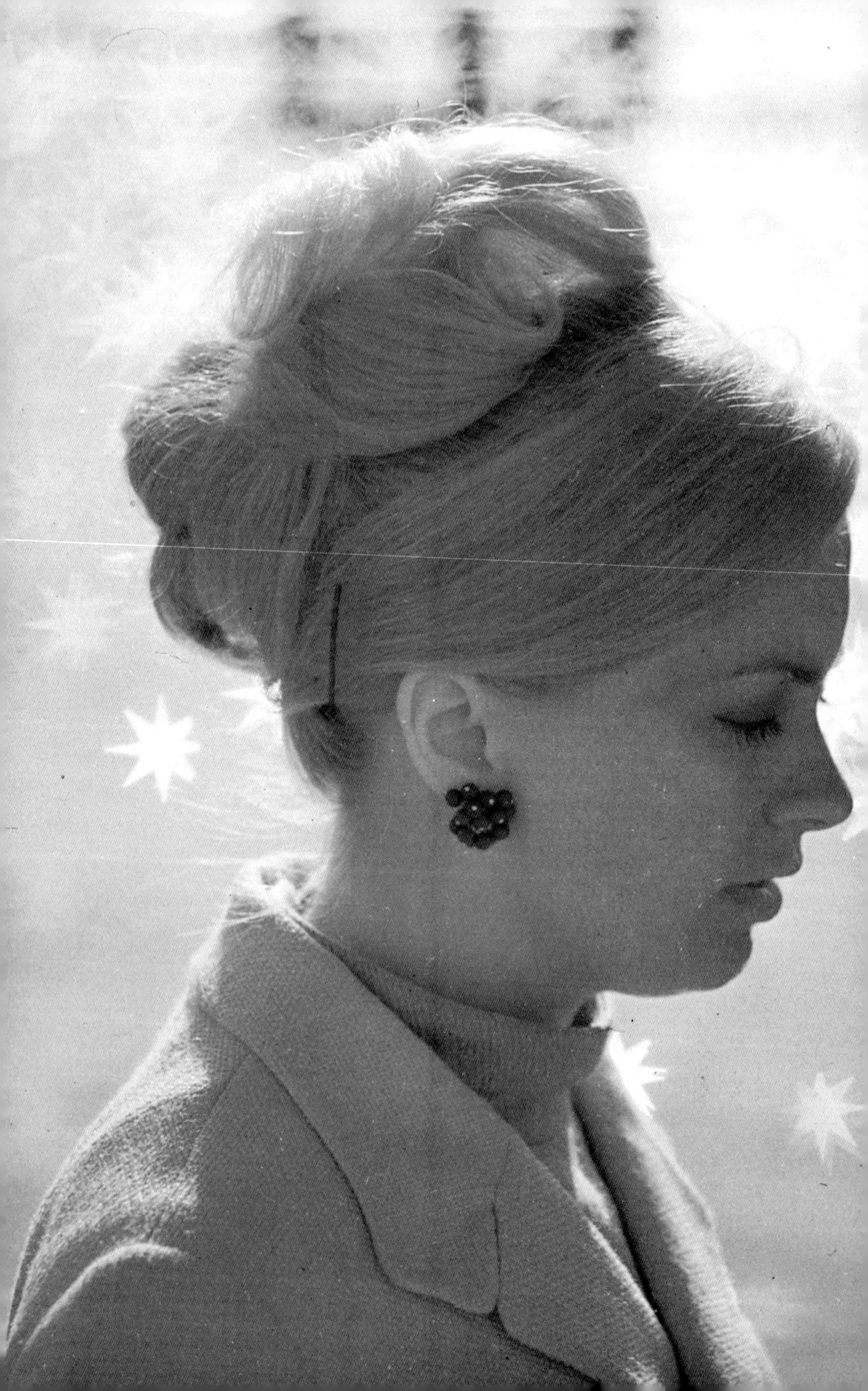

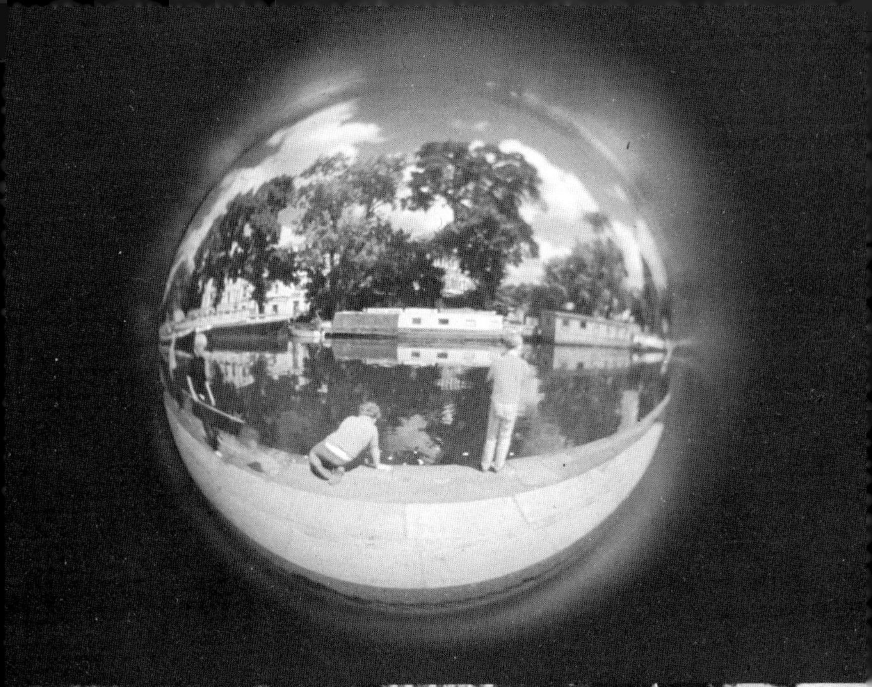

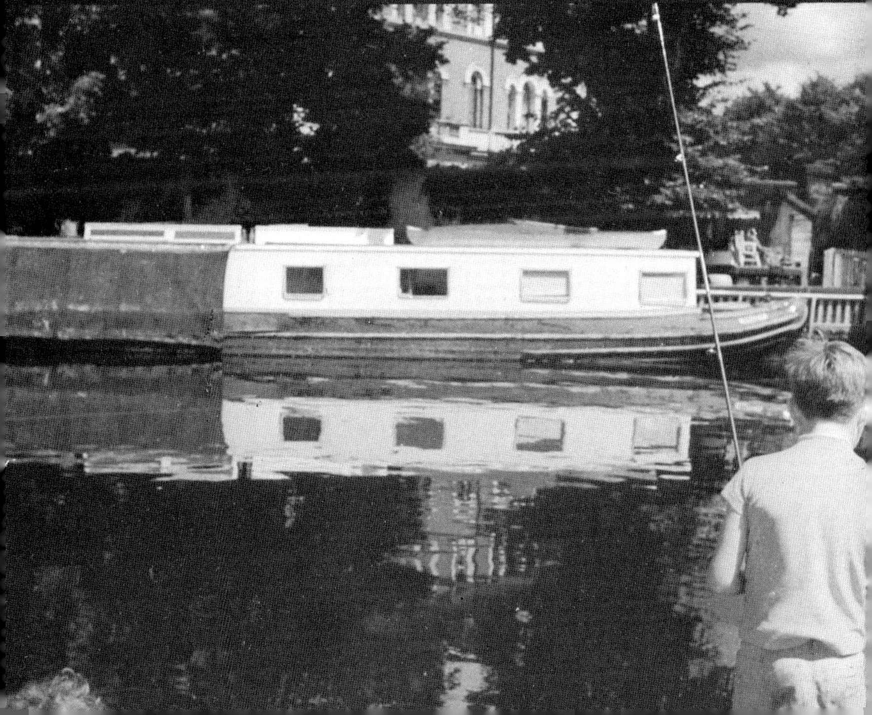

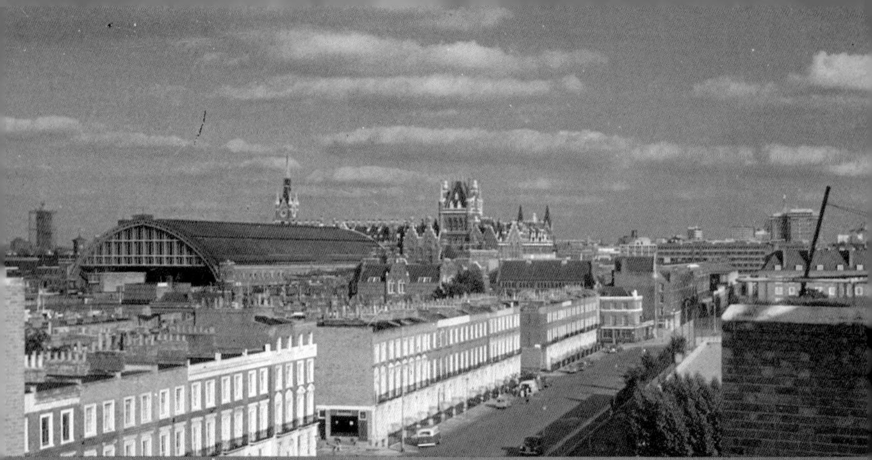

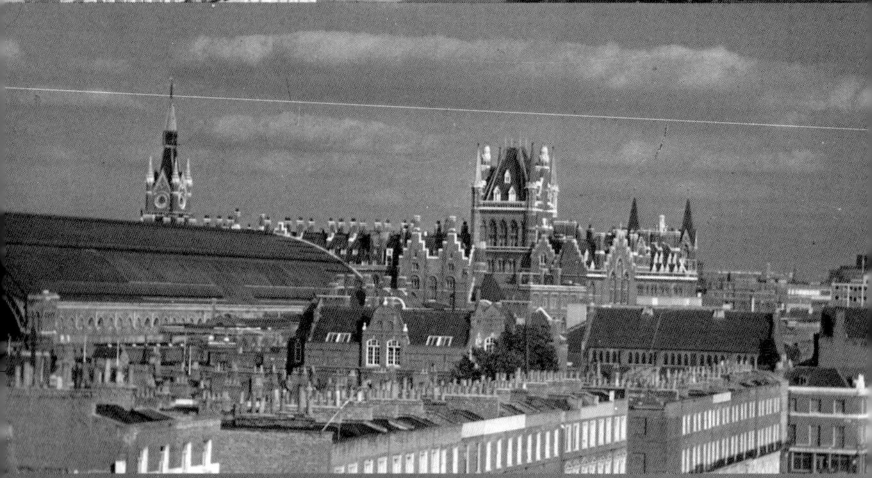

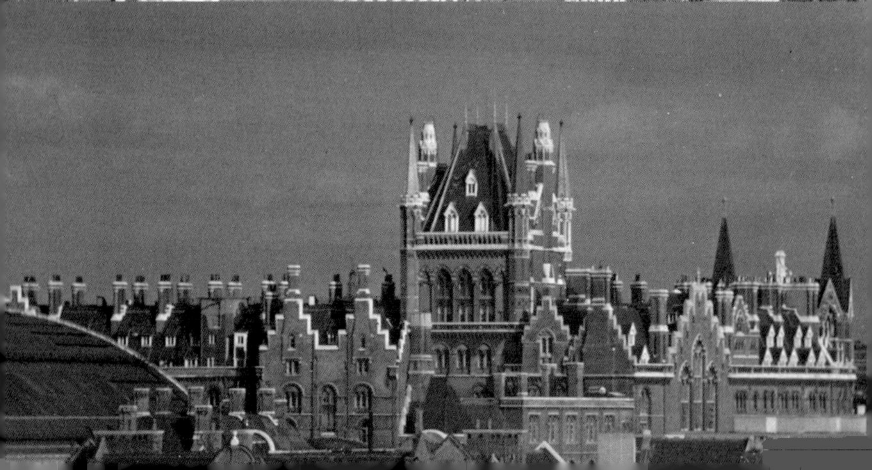

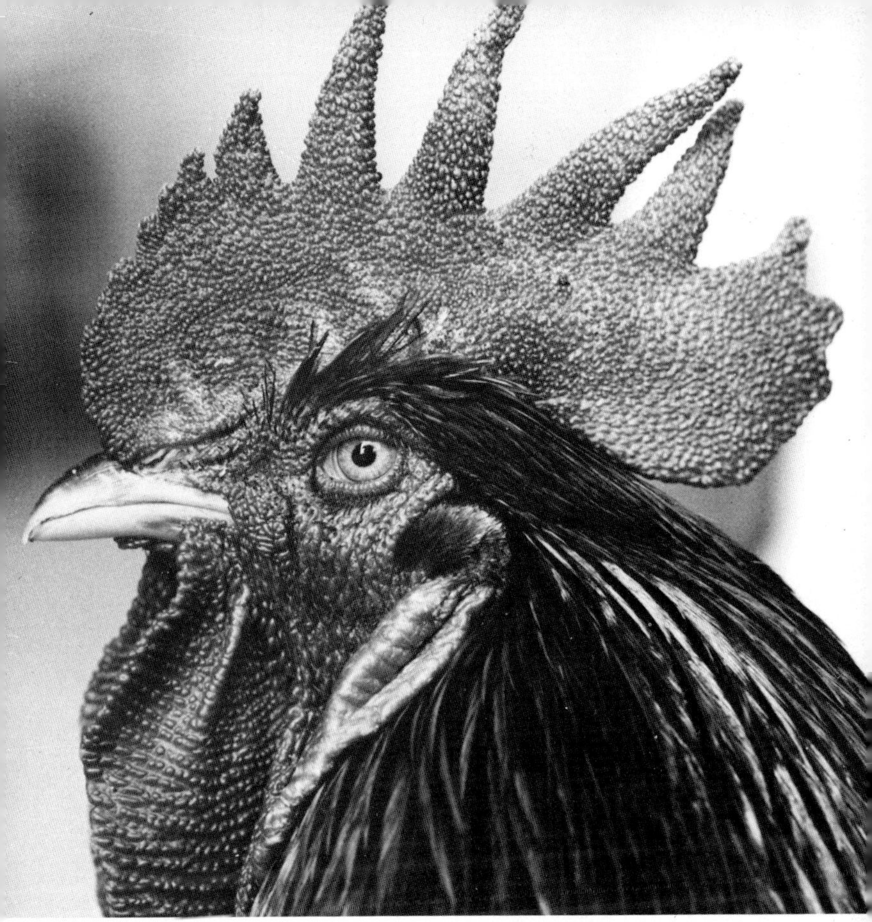

Above This close-up was taken with the aid of a bellows unit fitted between camera and lens. Exposure must be increased proportionally as the bellows are extended and the use of a tripod or other firm support is advisable, although this picture was taken hand-held. *Hasselblad, Jens Karlsson*

Opposite Fitting a teleconverter multiplies the effective focal length of the lens with which it is used. *Top* View with a 55 mm lens. *Centre* The same camera position but taken with a 55 mm lens plus 2x teleconverter, giving a combined focal length equivalent to 110 mm. *Bottom* 55 mm plus two 2x teleconverters, focal length equivalent to 220 mm. *Sidney Ray*

Previous page, top An inexpensive 'fish-eye' attachment can be made by fitting a clear 'spy-hole' into a piece of card and holding this in front of the camera's lens.

Previous page, bottom The above scene taken without the 'spy-hole' attachment. *Sidney Ray*

Overleaf Low light levels usually demand long exposures. A tripod is essential for shutter times longer than 1/30 sec especially when fine detail is to be resolved. *Rex Hayman*

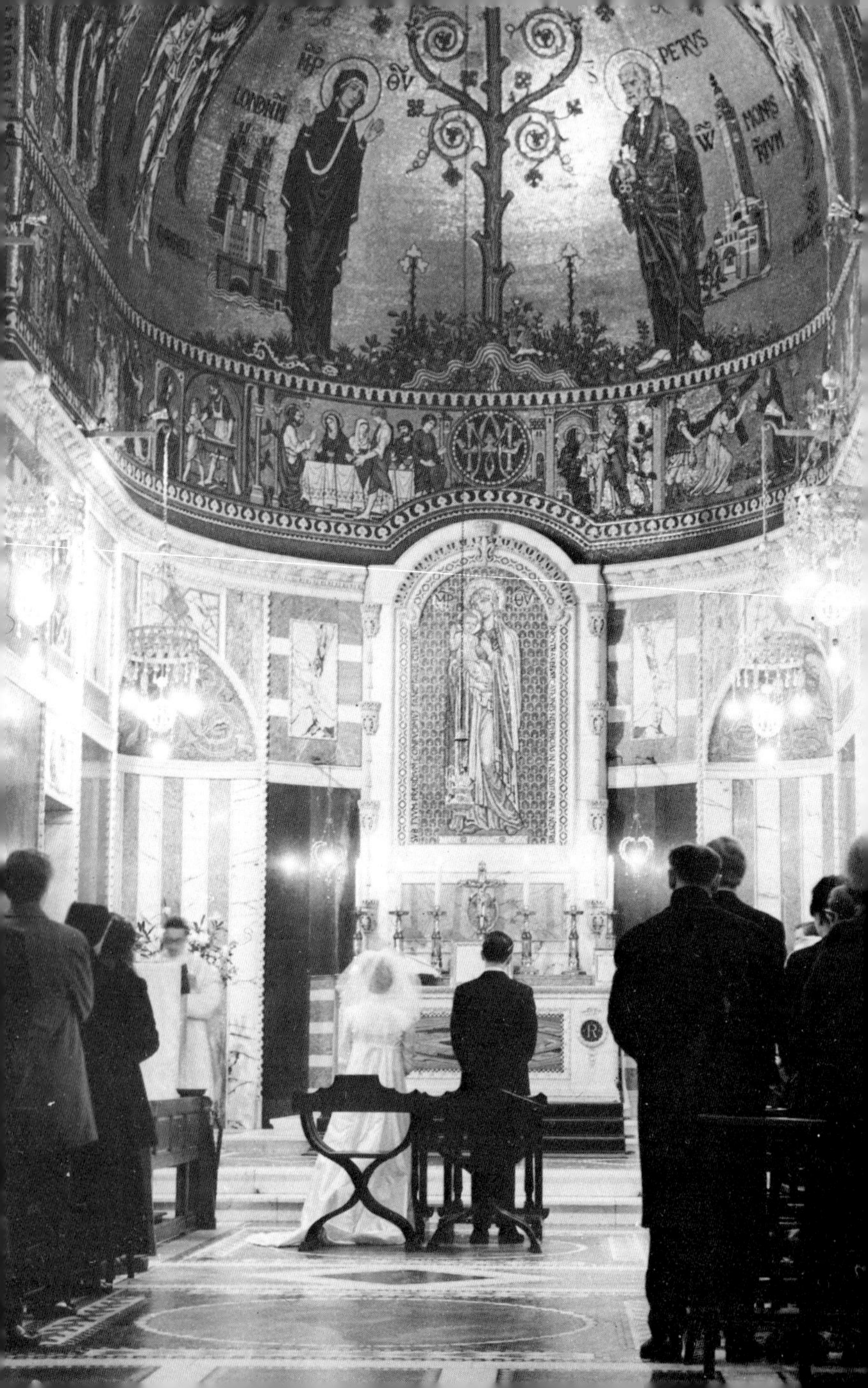
PETRVS

models have the disadvantages that they can be used automatically only when the flash unit is on or very close to the camera and for direct flash. If you bounce the flash off a wall, ceiling, etc. the sensor also points to the reflecting surface when it should be pointing at the subject.

Some units have a swivelling head, so that the sensor stays pointing at the subject no matter what the head fires at. You pay more for that. You pay still more for a remote sensor that can stay on the camera while the flash is used on a bracket or at a greater distance from the camera.

All automatic models can be switched to manual operation. Then you set the lens aperture according to the guide number and the distance. If you acquire an electronic flash unit without an instruction book, and you wish to know the guide number, simply multiply together any indicated pair of distance and aperture figures at the required film speed. Naturally, the guide number varies with film speed.

Finally, consider the power source. It must be an advantage to have a unit that can be operated from the domestic electricity supply as well as from the internal batteries. There must be some occasions when you want to use it indoors for close-up work, copying, etc. Adapters for this purpose are not expensive but they must be designed for the specific flash unit. Not all units have this capability.

Conversely, it is a definite disadvantage to have a unit with built-in rechargeable batteries. There are not too many of them about now, but there used to be a lot and their great diasadvantage was that when the battery needed recharging, the flash unit was out of commission for about 14 hours. If you forgot to recharge it after use, you could find it flat after two or three shots when you next needed it.

A few of the larger units available may still use the old lead-acid type of battery—like a miniature car battery. Avoid them unless you have a particular affinity for this type of battery because they need a lot of looking after. They are certainly not for the occasional user. Rechargeable nickel cadmium (nicad) batteries are popular but you must have at least two sets and they are quite expensive. They look just like the ordinary dry cell (AA is the usual size) but they give only 1.2 volts as against the normal 1.5. That can be a little low for some units. For most people, the alkaline battery is probably the best in the long run. They give a great many more flashes than the normal dry cell and have a far longer shelf life. They are a lot more expensive, too, but probably still the better value in the long run for flash guns.

The choice really boils down to power and price. If you intend to use flash regularly—and it has a lot of valid uses in close-up, copying, slide duplication, etc. even if you don't like it for normal work—get the highest power you can reasonably afford. Avoid the gimmicks unless you have a need for them. You don't need a swivelling head on a manual unit. You can probably buy a small ball and socket for less, or a flash bracket with swivelling facilities built in. Apart from that, you are likely to need two or more units if you begin to take flash work seriously. If you can afford it, go for the more professional types that allow for the attachment of extra heads and have switches to enable you to reduce the power. If cash is not readily available, buy a single unit with the idea in mind of buying others of the same type at a later date.

Flash accessories

There has been a tendency for some years now to produce a basic manufactured item and then to offer a variety of accessories to uprate it in performance, comfort, handling qualities, etc. The way is then wide open to independent manufacturers to design extras for your product. You can now buy filters, variable angle lenses, bounce reflectors, remote sensors, slave units, special battery packs, adapters of various kinds and so on. Some of these are specific branded items for particular units and you will learn all about them if you choose that type of unit, but there are a lot of accessories that have more genuine uses, some of which may be regarded as essential.

When you buy a flash unit you generally have just the basic caseful of works and tube with a contact in the foot and a cable so short that it may not even reach the socket on your camera. You can use it only on or very close to the camera. That is hardly the ideal place for any light source so you are compelled almost immediately to invest in accessories to enable you to operate the flash off the camera.

Off-camera flash accessories

The first essential for off-the-camera flash is an extension cord or lead. The synchronizing cord from the flash unit to the camera is generally very short—perhaps about 15 cm. You can buy extension cords with male and female connectors up to almost any length. The flash can then be operated at a distance from the camera governed only by the length of the cord or cords. If you become too ambitious you will eventually reach the point where the voltage drop over the cord will leave you with insufficient power to fire the tube but you are hardly likely to go that far. There are easier ways to fire a gun at a distance, as we shall indicate later. Generally, you require a cord of moderate length, up to 3 or 5 meters perhaps, to enable you to direct the light on to the subject at an angle. That gives better modelling and may throw the shadows out of the picture area. Spring-coiled leads; get tangled far less easily but cost more and are heavier.

Having taken care of the electrical connection, you then have to support the flash. If you want to move it only a short distance off camera to avoid the direct frontal effect and the possible infamous red-eye syndrome, you can use a flash bracket or bar. These come in a variety of forms. The simplest is a straight bar with a few holes in it, to accommodate a tripod screw, and with an accessory shoe fixed at one end. You attach the bar to the baseplate of the camera and slip the flash unit into the shoe. More elaborate types may be bent at one end to form a handle or at both ends to form two handgrips, with an accessory shoe atop one of them. The grips might have a cable release incorporated. The accessory shoe may be on a swivel or tilt mounting.

Flash bracket and hand grip are sometimes available separately, so that you can use the same handgrip with brackets designed for different cameras. A further development is an adjustable extension piece in the handgrip to raise the flash unit between 30 and 50 cm above the camera. A similar product attaches to the camera tripod socket and raises the flash a fixed 38 cm.

When you want the flash further away from the camera than any bracket can allow, you can improvise simply by standing it on a table, shelf, etc. or by persuading a friend to hold it for you. Greater security is obtained by using a tripod, camera clamp or similar camera support to hold the flash unit. As these items are generally equipped only with a tripod screw, you need another little accessory; an accessory shoe mounted on a block with a tripod bush.

Making multiple flash easier

A single flash unit tends to provide highly directional light leading to harsh shadows. When you take the flash off the camera to improve modelling, you may find part of the subject distractingly under-illuminated. You can solve that problem reasonably well by using reflectors and/or bounced flash techniques, but full lighting, especially on the background, can be obtained only by using more than one flash source. The additional sources can be extra heads that plug into the power pack of the main unit, but the average user is likely to use complete units in each location. The problem then is to fire each unit in synchronism. There are two ways of doing that—with and without extension cords.

Most cameras have both accessory shoe terminals and cord sockets and sometimes both can be used together. Then two units can be fired in synchronism. In other cases, or where more than two units are used, the cords have somehow to be connected together. Multi-way sockets are freely available. You push them into the flash socket on the camera and push the flash unit cords into the two or three other sockets thus provided.

Unfortunately, the straightforward adaptors of this kind are not foolproof, particularly when the flash units used on them are not identical.

They could have different polarities or different firing voltages, resulting in erratic firing or firing of one unit when the other is connected. It is not impossible for damage to be caused to both flash unit and shutter contacts. A more sophisticated adapter is available incorporating a safety circuit to take care of such incompatibilities.

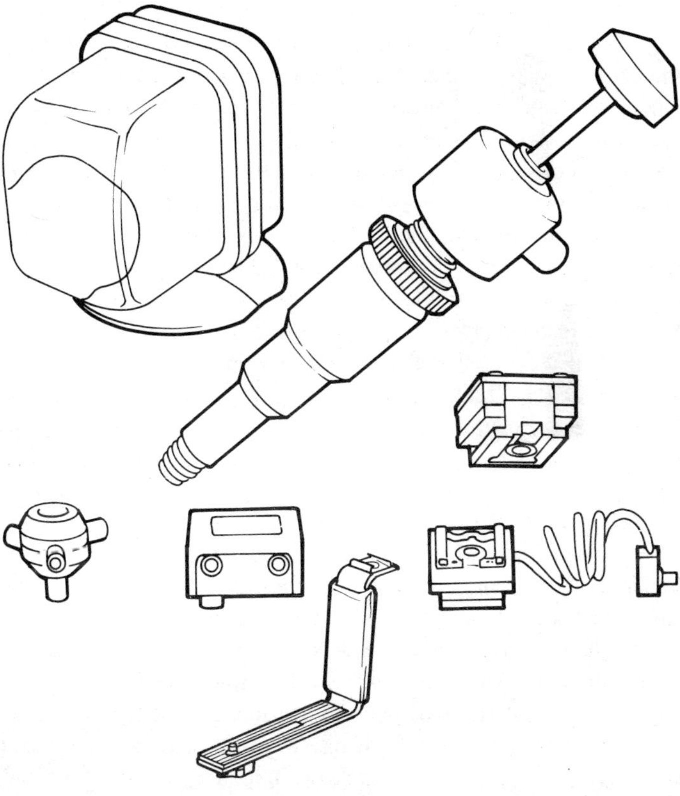

There are innumerable flash accessories, including (*from top down*) slave unit, external synchronizer, tripod-mounting accessory shoe, multi-sockets, flash bracket, and hot-shoe adapter.

Whatever kind of adapter you use, you may have a considerable problem with trailing leads, particularly if you want to use a full lighting set-up with three or four units. If you shoot from 3 m or so with a flash on the camera, another to one side for modelling and another on the background, you could need to be very nimble to avoid pulling the whole set-up down about your ears. This is inevitable sooner or later.

There is an easy and not too expensive way out of this difficulty. The problem is to fire the remote flashes without cords leading back to the camera. That is a simple matter indeed for modern electronic techniques. All you need is a light-operated switch—one that will close instantaneously with any sudden increase in light level. Such switches have been in use for years and have been adapted to photography in the form of slave units. It is possible to find quite inexpensive ones.

A very efficient type is also the least expensive. It consists of a light sensor and three or four other tiny components embedded in transparent casting resin with a flash socket incorporated and a suction cup attached. It measures about $2.5 \times 1.5 \times 1.5$ cm. You plug the flash unit sync cord into it and stick it on the side of the flash unit. You can then place this slave-controlled unit in the required position and it will fire instantaneously when the sensor receives light from the flash attached to the camera. Of course, you can use as many slaves as you like. Generally you should place them so that their sensors face the master flash but these types and most others too, are now so sensitive that they will fire, at least in a small room, when the sensor faces one wall and the master flash faces the wall oposite. They also work at extraordinary distances (12–15 m is not uncommon), even in daylight. Naturally this depends on the power of the activating flash, which should not normally have a guide number less than about 30 (metres) for 100ASA film. Smaller units will operate the slave but at much reduced distances. The most convenient place for the master flash is on your camera; or on a flash bar. In most cases you can treat this as the fill-in flash in your set up, adjusting it and the other units so that the lighting ratio is right. However, if you do not want any light from the camera direction, face your flash to one side, so that all it does is fire the slave units.

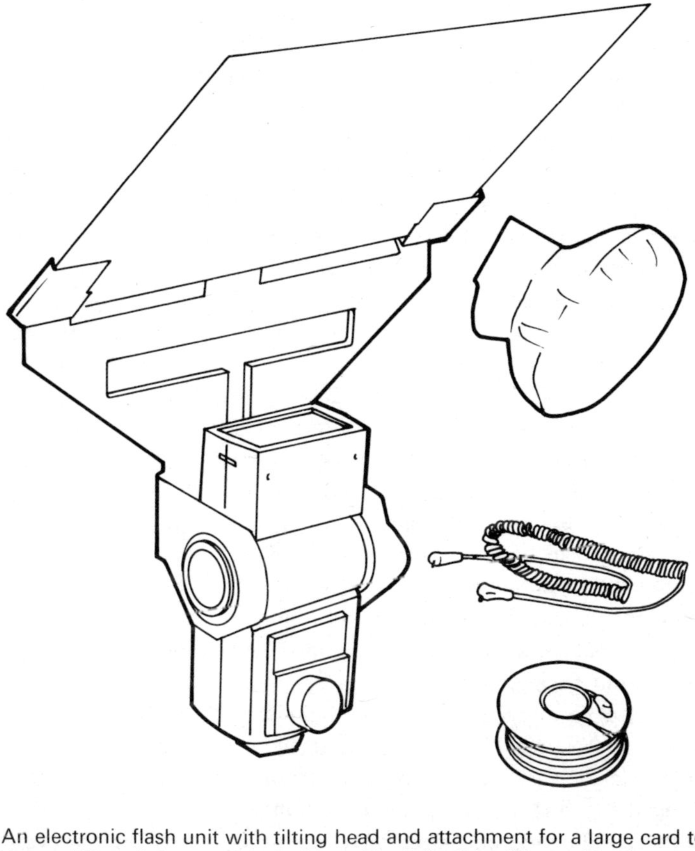

An electronic flash unit with tilting head and attachment for a large card to throw diffuse light on to the subject. The inflatable diffuser (*right*) comes with six colour filters. Extension flash leads for off camera work are available in various lengths. They may be straight, coiled or wound on a reel.

Attachments for diffused lighting

Multiple flash and, to some extent, off-camera flash in general, are for the studio or a reasonably static set-up. If you are moving around with the camera and have to use your flash on or close to it, an indirect technique may avoid the harsh, flat lighting characteristic of such work.

Indirect lighting implies the use of a reflecting surface off which you bounce the light on to the subject. It thus becomes more diffuse and covers a larger area. The intensity on the subject is, of course, reduced, so the technique is usable only with units of reasonable power.

It is not really necessary to buy reflectors for this. Most rooms have white ceilings that are fine for this purpose. They need to be white or neutral-coloured when you work with colour. With that proviso you can bounce your flash off any surface within range but it is undoubtedly convenient, especially when working outdoors, to carry your reflector with you.

These, too, come in many forms. Folding types are readily available. Generally white, they can also have silver or gold-coloured surfaces for particular purposes. The gold colour is said to give a suitable 'warming up' effect to shots taken on dull days. A rigid type about one metre square comes with a lightweight tripod.

The brolly flash is a similar idea used in a rather different way. The flat reflector is used with direct flash to throw light into shadow areas. Or it can be used with bounced flash with relatively small subjects. The brolly flash is used as a light source in itself. A common type incorporates a tripod mounting for a more or less conventional umbrella with white or silvered inner surface. The flash is mounted pointing into the opened brolly and away from the subject so that the light is bounced but to some extent directed back to the subject. The result is a cross between diffuse and directional lighting. Other forms are more elaborate with heavy tripod stands and, perhaps, modelling lights.

All these reflector units are portable and easily moved around even when erected but for true manoeuvrability a simpler device has to be used. Such a device is incorporated into some 'system' flash units with swivelling heads. The reflector takes the form of a standard grey card with a white surface on the other side. It clips into a support attached to the flash unit so that the head can be tilted up to fire at the white surface which is angled to direct a reasonably diffused light on to the subject.

An ingenious device known as an air diffuser consists of a plastic bag construction that fits over the average smaller flashgun and inflates to provide a bulbous diffuse light source.

A minor accessory that can be useful if you have no other means of angling your flash is a ball-and-socket mount with foot to fit an accessory shoe and a shoe at the top on a rather longer stalk than usual. The flash unit can then be tilted in any required direction.

Miscellaneous accessories

Most of the accessories we have mentioned so far involve the use of extension cords. As we have said these are freely available in various lengths. You are likely to need more than one unless you work exclusively with slave units. You could buy only one long cord, say 5 m or more, in the belief that it will serve all your needs, particularly if it is the coiled type that stetches to its full length only when necessary. But the probability is that you will do a lot of work with the flash unit much closer to the camera, say on a bracket. You then have a lot of cord to dispose of when you need only a few centimetres. It is advisable, in fact, always to have a very short cord, just enough for flash bracket work, with the other or others tailored to your expected requirements.

Look at the cord carefully before you buy it, especially if it is a long one. It should be reasonably stout with solidly moulded fittings because it will have to stand up to rough usage when trailing around the floor. It is a lucky man who never catches his foot in a trailing flash lead. That is largely why slave units are preferable.

Some flash units have separate plug-in cords to be used only when required. So universal has the foot contact become that some units are even supplied without a cord. You will need one and it will cost extra. Watch out for these proprietary types. They often use special plugs and sockets and when you buy one you must be sure that you get the right one. Do not rely on the salesman even if you quote the name. The standard camera flash socket is a 3 mm coaxial and adaptors are available for some of the non-standard types.

An accessory not so commonly needed now is the foot contact (hot shoe type) to cord adapter. This fits into the hot shoe of cameras so equipped and provides a socket for cord-only type flash units. There are now few cameras without both types of contact, however. The opposite arrangement is also now uncommon—the foot contact flash unit with no cable. If you have one, and a camera with no hot shoe, an adapter with cord attached fits onto the flash unit foot and then into the accessory shoe. The cord can then be plugged in to the camera socket.

Another comparatively rare accessory is the external flash synchronizer. All modern cameras have synchronized shutters but if you should use an older camera without this facility, you can buy a synchronizer that screws into the cable release socket. It has a socket for the flash lead and a plunger that operates both the shutter release and a flash switch. Careful adjustment is necessary for each camera and spot-on synchronization at higher speeds can be difficult.

Flash exposure meters

So far we have not dealt to any extent with studio equipment. This is partly because most readers are likely to be interested in the less expensive equipment and also because studio set-ups tend to come complete from one manufacturer. Detailed information is readily available in technical literature and publicity material.

Had this book been written a few years ago, it is likely that this section would not have appeared either. Exposure meters for flash work have been available for many years but they used to be cumbersome, not completely reliable and very expensive. Progress in electronic technology is now so rapid, however, that a practical flashmeter can be obtained for a lot less than some continuous light meters—and prices are still falling.

A flashmeter is basically a very simple instrument in terms of the job it has to do. It has only to measure the light falling on it and indicate a lens aperture for correct exposure. The problem arises, of course, in finding electronic components to react fast enough to

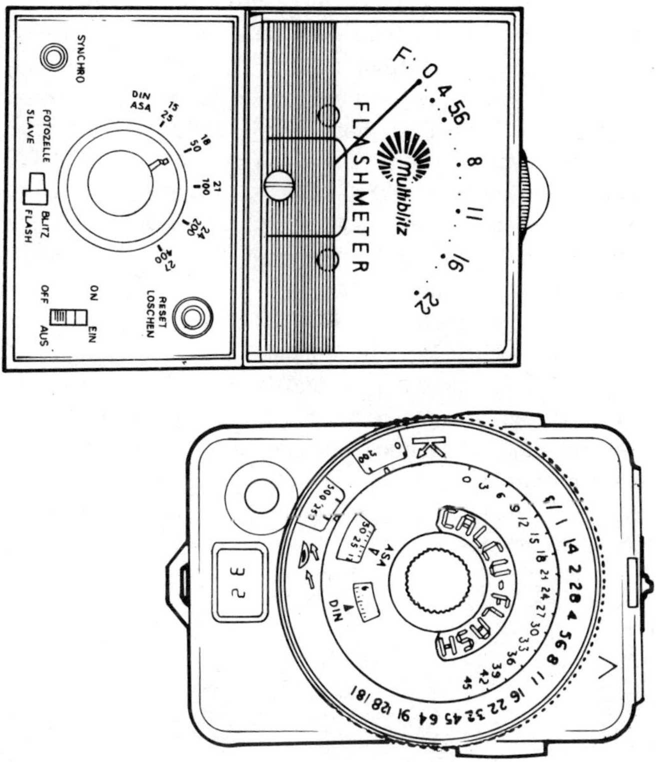

Flash meters are activated simultaneously with the flash and give a reading of the aperture required for correct exposure. The traditional type use a needle and scale. The all-electronic versions give a digital readout to be translated on scaled dials.

measure the flash and translate it into a reading. The reaction time has to be no slower than 1/1000 second and, now that we have the incredibly short duration of some automatic units, it should be much, much faster. That is now relatively easily accomplished and flash meters are well within the reach of many hobby photographers.

The most inexpensive models are naturally less versatile than those that still cost rather more, but they may soon be forced off the market by a steady fall in price of the most advanced models. An average-priced unit may not react faster than about 1/5000 second. It measures only the flash, cannot accumulate flashes and needs to be switched from high to low range according to sensitivity. It may use a moving needle giving occasionally indistinct readings on a compressed scale, and so on.

Already, however, at a price below that of, for example, almost all 35 mm SLR cameras, a flash meter is available with an extraordinary specification. It measures both ambient light and flash and can be used in incident or reflected light modes. It holds the reading and adds further flashes to it if required. Normally, it is auto ranging, i.e. it switches itself to a less sensitive range as necessary. An attenuator is nevertheless provided for 'super-high' illumination. The readout is a two-figure LED display used in conjunction with a large, easily read calculator dial. The reading is turned off after 60 seconds but can be recalled by pressing a memory button. A cord from the meter to the flash unit allows manual firing. Reaction time is such that no normal electronic flash is too fast for measurement.

Lighting Equipment

Continuous artificial light sources (incandescent lamps, as opposed to flash) are less popular than they were a few years ago. Many studios have turned over entirely to the sophisticated but compact electronic flash systems now available. They offer so many advantages in intensity for size, colour temperature, ease of movement, lack of trailing cables, particularly where slave units are used, reliability, lack of heat, and choice of materials. More spontaneity is often called for in some studio work now and flash undoubtedly helps in that direction, too.

Nevertheless, there is still a lot of lighting equipment about and many people are using it for still photography. The hobby photographer, in particular, does not find it easy to use multiple flash set-ups. For him, the necessary equipment with modelling lights and flash meter is prohibitively expensive, whereas photolamps and reflectors can cost relatively little.

Tungsten lighting is widely used for black-and-white work, probably rather less for colour negative and very little for colour slides. There are few colour slide materials suitable for tungsten lighting and those that are available are designed for studio lamps and not the overrun photofloods that used to be so popular with amateurs.

Tungsten lamps

The ordinary tungsten lamp, as used in the household, is quite suitable for black-and-white photography and there is even a case for using 150 or 200 watt versions to avoid the harsh, overlit effect of photofloods used too closely. They are quite powerful enough with modern fast films and wide-aperture lenses.

The type of lighting you use, however, does rather depend on your kind of work. If you aim at pin-sharp full or three-quarter length portraits, room interiors, close-ups of small items, etc. you might need to shoot at small apertures. That can be enough to make more powerful lighting preferable and if, in addition, you prefer not to use the slightly coarser fast films, then you certainly need to consider photofloods.

Photofloods are available in two basic forms. The pearl type (not to be confused with photopearls) looks much like an ordinary domestic lamp and is used in a reflector bowl or dish. The reflector photoflood is similar in appearance to the so-called domestic spotlights and window-display lights. It has a built-in reflector that gives a good forward throw of light without external assistance.

There are two popular sizes: Nos 1 and 2. They consume 275 and 500 watts respectively but give considerably more light than would normally be expected from such ratings—perhaps in the region of 650 and 1250 watts. That is achieved by overrunning, i.e. by making the filament burn at a much higher temperature than in an ordinary lamp and so give more light. You have to pay for that with a shorter life—about 3 hours for the No 1 and 6 hours for the No 2.

Both bayonet and screw fittings are available for the pearl types but reflector floods are supplied only with screw fitting.

Photofloods are not really suitable for colour photography. They give a rather bluer light (colour temperature 3400 K) than available tungsten light films are designed for. They are therefore declining in popularity in favour of the photopearl type with a colour temperature of 3200 K. Theoretically, photofloods should work well enough with colour negative film, but the results may not come out too well with machine printing. There are special long-exposure colour negative films which *are* designed for tungsten. Also, in some countries colour movie film in 35 mm cassettes is available. This, too, is usually balanced for tungsten lighting.

Photopearls are not so heavily overrun as photofloods. They consume 500 watts to give the equivalent of about 800–900 watts. They cost a lot more than photofloods but have a life of 100 hours. A very large 1000 watt version and a 500 watt type with internal reflector are also available. Photopearls, sometimes called 100 hour photofloods, are supplied in screw fitting only.

The non-reflector lamps, photopearl and photoflood, are commonly used in reflectors of various shapes to give the quality of light required. The popular form of reflector for a No 1 photoflood was, for some years, a spun aluminium type about 6 in deep to the lampholder and about 7 in in diameter at the front. It is still supplied and gives a hard, directional light. Other designs are now freely available and, at the other extreme is a 21 in diameter very shallow dish with white surface and a baffle plate suspended in the centre in front of the lamp. Virtually all light is provided indirectly by the reflector to give a soft, diffused effect.

Tungsten halogen lamps

Ordinary tungsten lamps have a glass envelope filled at relatively low pressure with an inert gas. The tungsten filament gradually burns away and deposits form on the glass envelope, causing blackening and an alleged lowering of colour temperature. (It is more likely to be due to the loss of luminous efficiency in the decaying filament.) Tungsten-halogen lamps incorporate a halogen in the gas filling that reacts in a complicated manner with the incandescent tungsten to prolong its life, prevent envelope blackening, enable higher pressures and temperatures to be used and, above all, to increase luminous efficiency for a given wattage.

Generally speaking, therefore, tungsten halogen lamps give a brighter, whiter light and have a longer life than overrun studio lamps. They are relatively expensive because the higher temperature and gas pressure require a quartz or special glass envelope that is easily damaged by finger marks. As this type of lamp develops, however, double envelopes with glass protecting the quartz inner envelope are becoming more common. Tungsten halogen lamps are gradually replacing the ordinary tungsten lamps in studio lighting units, which can be made more compact as a result.

Various studio lighting heads are designed for tungsten halogen lamps from 650 up to 5000 watts and more. A common 650 watt type gives more light than a 500 watt photoflood and has a life of 75 hours. The 5000 watt type gives about 8 times as much light and has a life of 400 hours. Connections are usually bi-post, or double-ended for tubular types.

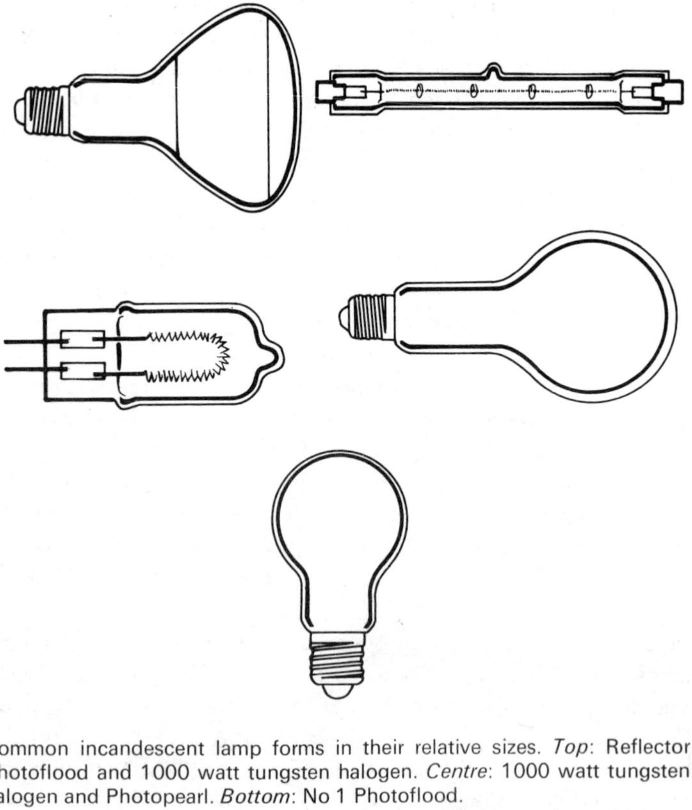

Common incandescent lamp forms in their relative sizes. *Top*: Reflector Photoflood and 1000 watt tungsten halogen. *Centre*: 1000 watt tungsten halogen and Photopearl. *Bottom*: No 1 Photoflood.

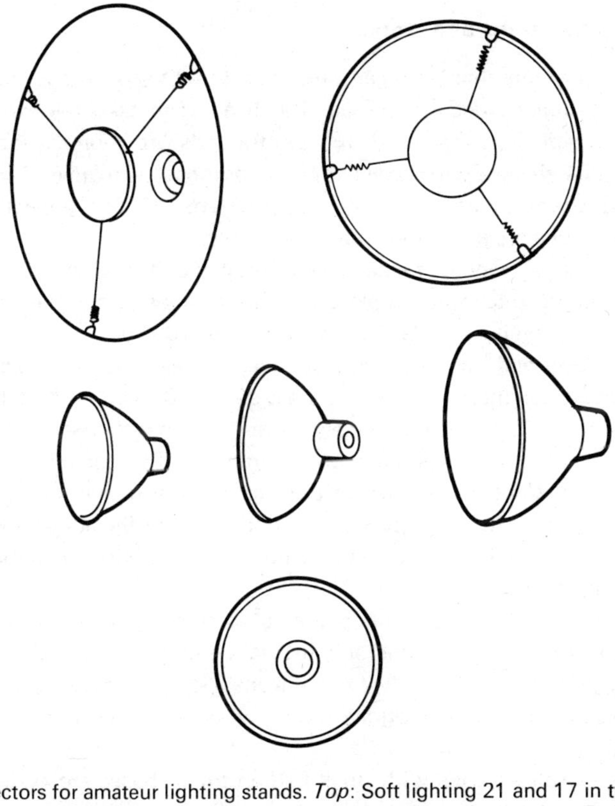

Reflectors for amateur lighting stands. *Top*: Soft lighting 21 and 17 in types with baffle. *Centre*: 7, 9 and 11 in reflectors for contrastier lighting. *Bottom*: Middle of the road 13 in type without baffle.

Lamp units for tungsten halogen lamps generally need careful fusing. With the wrong fuse, they can cause heavy arcing when the filament finally burns out. The heat generated can shatter the envelope with dangerous force. Similar results can occur from overvolting, undue vibration (by moving the lamp when it is switched on) or overheating. Most good quality units are supplied with wire guards and more than adequate ventilation, sometimes by fan. Nevertheless, every possible precaution against shattering should be taken and fuses should never be improvised or replaced by ones with higher ratings.

Lamp housings and stands

Most photographic lamps are designed to be used in lamp heads or housings carried on stands. The heads can take the form of simple reflectors as used for photofloods or more elaborate housings designed basically for two purposes—to give either a broad beam of light or a concentrated patch. The generalized descriptions are flood and spot respectively.

The housings vary from small easily portable units weighing a mere kilogram or so to, for example, a 68 x 43 cm housing for three 1500 watt tungsten halogen lamps weighing in at 10 kilos.

Both flood and spot types are supplied with various accessories. The most common accessory is a set of barn doors—opaque flaps fixed to two or all four sides of the housing (most tungsten halogen type housings are now rectangular). The barn doors can be swung toward the front of the unit to control the amount of light that is allowed to spill on to various parts of the subject. Barn doors for spotlights (generally with a circular lens) can be in rotating form.

The simplest reflectors can be on clamps or small stands with clamps incorporated. Little serious work can be done with these however because they rely on the availability of surfaces or edges for standing or clamping at the right height and in the right position.

More versatile stands with small folding tripod bases are available at reasonable prices. A popular type is made from lightweight metal tubing in two sections extending to 1.8 m (6 ft) with a base

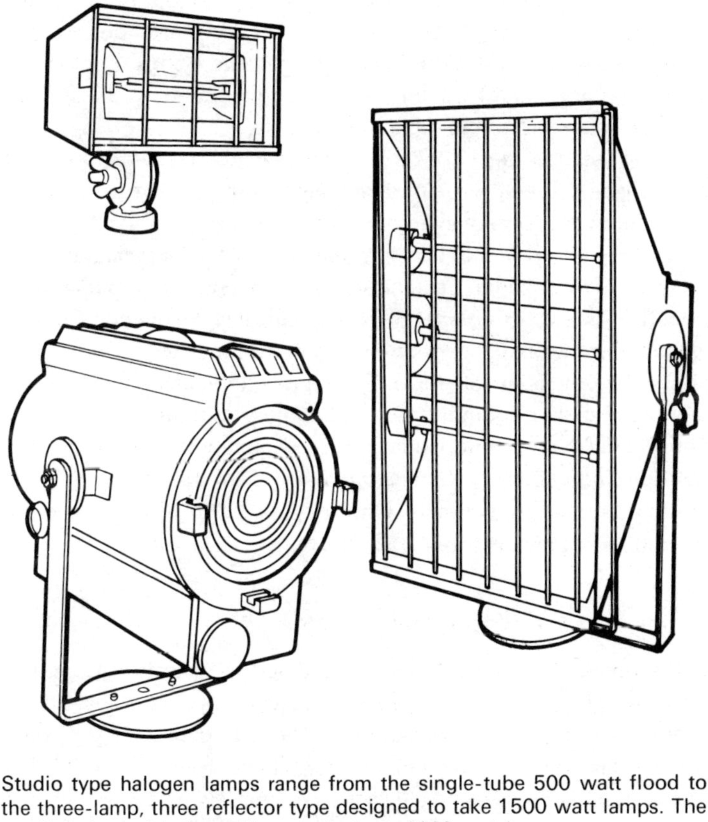

Studio type halogen lamps range from the single-tube 500 watt flood to the three-lamp, three reflector type designed to take 1500 watt lamps. The spotlight has a 6 in fresnel lens and takes a 1000 watt lamp.

spread of about 78 cm or 30 in. This, and larger sizes in the same range, is basically a domestic type with its own system of attachments such as a lampholder unit to take a range of reflectors and a brolly flash set-up. Similar, but sturdier, units are supplied for studio or location use with lightweight reflectors and photopearl or photoflood lamps.

The heavier lighting units need sturdier supports and a degree of standardization. These supports generally take the form of heavy three or four leg wheel bases designed to accept 35 mm diameter tubing as the main stem. Tubular inserts with a variety of fittings give the required extension and a rapid lamphouse attachment.

The standard international fitting is now a $\frac{5}{8}$ in spigot on the stand taking a tubular fitting with clamp wheel on the lamp housing. The British Standard type still widely used has the clamp tube on the stand and the spigot on the lamp housing. Adapters to convert from one standard to the other are available.

Lighting stands are generally designed to take a range of accessories. Several types of attachment to the vertical column are provided in the form of swinging sleeves and arms, and clamps for tubes fixed at an angle. Leg brackets allow low level lamps to be fitted to the horizontal, rectangular-section legs. Boom arms are a popular fitment, of course, allowing lamps to be manoeuvred at various distances and height without moving the stand.

In some cases, relatively fixed lighting positions can be catered for by wall or ceiling mountings. A ceiling mounting may take a lamp house directly or, more usually, jointed arms with extension and 360° turning capability. Similar movements are possible with wall-mounted units but, naturally, with only a 180° turn. The maximum turning radius may extend to 1.5 or 2 m.

Choosing your lighting equipment

In the domestic situation, you are confined to occasionally setting up your lighting in a room generally used for other purposes. You cannot go for too sophisticated a set-up, particularly if your storage capacity is also limited. You have to use one of the lightweight pack-away systems or perhaps even resort to small stand or clamp units.

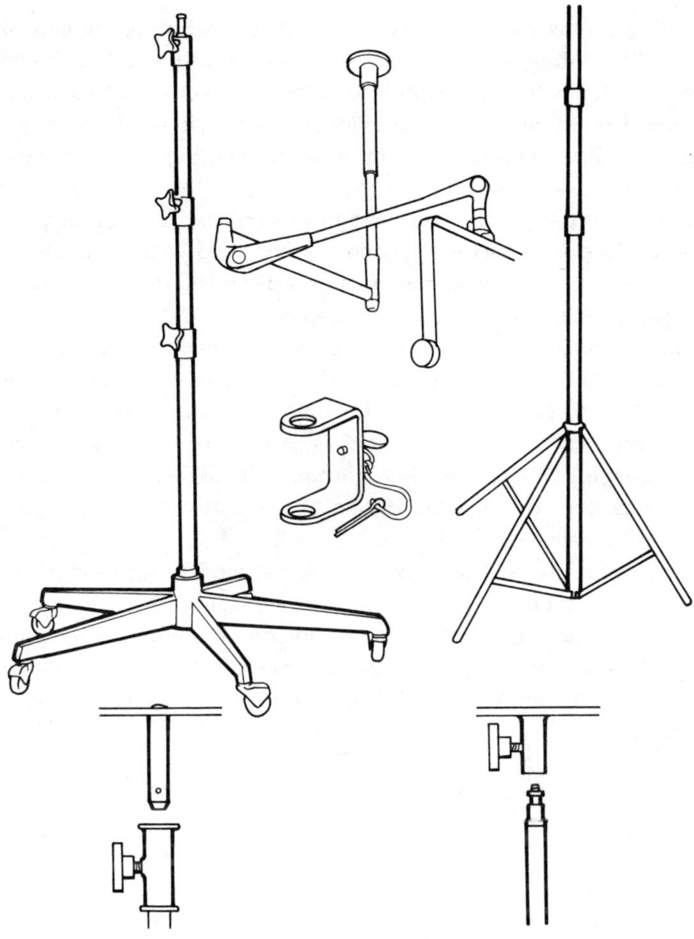

Studio stands can be the relatively heavy wheeled type or the lightweight folding type popular on location. They may be fitted with the British 5/8 in spigot (*bottom, left*) or the International 5/8 in fitting (*right*). The leg bracket (*centre*) allows lamps to be mounted on a stand leg or other 2 × 1 in rectangular tube. *Top*: a versatile ceiling mounting.

Folding stands are more versatile but they need a fair amount of room. If you buy those with a limited base spread, you have to be very careful with the height and balance of your lighting head. Using a boom arm can be hazardous. All this is the fault of the location rather than the product. It has to be designed with space considerations in mind.

Many such designs are available from suppliers to both amateur and professional markets. Location stands need to be rugged but easily portable and most manufacturers of professional equipment supply them at quite reasonable prices.

Lightweight stands may yet prove to be more versatile as tungsten halogen lighting units improve. They are becoming smaller, more powerful and better balanced. They are expensive, inevitably, but the life of some of the later units is way beyond that of normal photographic lamps. There is, for example, a 1500 watt, 2000 hour unit available with standard fitting at the cost of about eight or nine photopearl lamps.

If your are taking indoor work with full lighting set-ups seriously—and have the necessary storage space—take a look at a lighting specialist's catalogue before you decide on your equipment. A lot of their stuff is very expensive but a surprising amount is available at prices that compare very well with those ruling on the 'amateur' market.

Supporting the Camera

When you take a photograph, you allow the light reflected from the subject to pass through the camera lens on to the film. When the subject is moving, the image on the film moves, too, so you have to select a fast shutter speed to 'stop' the movement and get a sharp picture. Everybody understands that: if the subject moves, the image moves. Not everybody seems to appreciate that the image on the film also moves if the camera moves. Or, if they do, they believe it can't happen to them.

We all know the person who can get perfectly sharp pictures at 1/8 second or even slower and never uses a tripod. He is rather like the one who never gets grain on 20×16 in blow-ups from a quarter of a 35 mm negative. Even in carefully controlled conditions it is virtually impossible to hold a camera *absolutely* steady for 1/8 second. Not many people can hand-hold with perfect confidence at 1/30 second, and it is even possible to suffer camera shake at 1/1000 second, especially with a focal plane shutter.

So there is a case to be made out for a tripod as the least used but most essential photographic accessory. Lenses, films and chemistry are now at such a stage of development that most images produced by photographers are less sharp, in absolute terms, than they could be. Fortunately, even the best human eyesight is far from perfect and the lack of absolute sharpness may not be detectable at the normal 25 cm or greater viewing distance. So we can happily shoot at shutter speeds of 1/125 second and faster with reasonable certainty of sharp results. With care, we can manage 1/60 second. Slower than that and *some* loss of sharpness is inevitable.

All that assumes a well-balanced camera and lens assembly of no more than moderate focal length (say 135 mm, or perhaps up to a compact 200 mm on a 35 mm camera). As the angle of view becomes narrower, it takes only a fractional movement of the camera to displace the image considerably.

For the sharpest pictures, and sometimes for any real sharpness at all, the camera should be on some form of rigid support whenever a shutter speed slower than 1/30 second is used or the lens focal length is more than about four times the standard focal length. In many cases, even stricter limits could apply.

Tripods

The best all-round camera support is a tripod—but it could also be the worst. To be efficient a tripod must have a reasonable weight and bulk, and thereby becomes rather inconvenient and conspicuous in use. Those disadvantages alone are enough to make the sight of a photographer carrying a tripod one of the rarities of our time. There is, additionally, a certain lack of elegance in a tripod: it spoils the Cartier-Bresson image, or that of the modern photojournalist.

If you can overcome these ego-trip barriers, you could use a tripod often. A well-designed tripod can ease your task considerably in many circumstances. Any kind of architectural photography benefits from careful lining up of the subject and critical sharpness. Both are easier to attain with the camera independently mounted.

A great deal of sports photography can be, and is, carried out from a tripod. You often concentrate on one particular area of the track or field and, once the camera is lined up, you have little need to use the viewfinder again. You know your lens angle and you can watch the shot coming up. There is the telling, probably apocryphal, story of the cricket specialist who never watched the game. His reflexes were trained to press the cable release instantaneously with the shouted appeals.

Many portraits, figure studies, etc. would be better shot from a tripod. You can communicate much better with your model face to face than through the camera body or the top of your head. With a suitably long cable release you can even sit facing your subject with the camera shooting over your shoulder.

A tripod must be chosen with care. The fact that it extends to 2 m or more is not much use to you unless you intend to carry a step-ladder as well. The popular rising centre column has limited uses unless it is about 75 mm thick. Multi-joints allowing the whole assembly to collapse into a jacket pocket can be less than

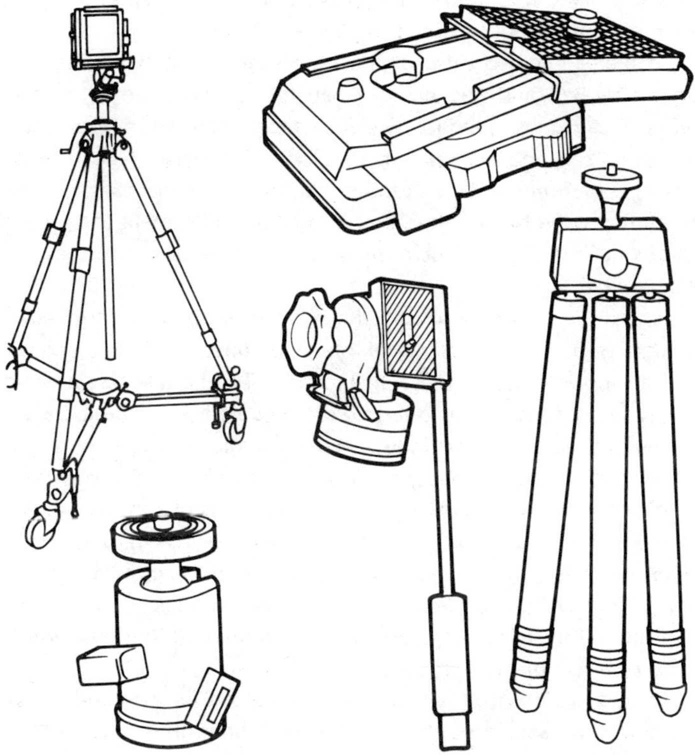

Tripods vary from heavy studio versions on wheels to collapsing portable types in many sizes and strengths. The camera can be attached to a pan-tilt head with long operating handle or a simpler ball-and-socket mounting. For rapid camera attachment to either, mating clip and shoe (*top right*) can be attached to camera and tripod respectively.

advantageous if the joints form also multiple centres of vibration. The efficient tripod has a modest height, 150 cm being about the practical limit for a portable, as oposed to a transportable, model. It may have a centre column extending some 50 cm further, but that should be used only in dire necessity. Strong, lightweight metals are available now, but the legs must be of sufficient cross section to offer fair resistance to bending at the bottom joint under hand pressure. The locks must be absolutely secure in all positions, resisting all attempts to press the assembly down from the top. Reversible feet with rubber plugs on one side and spikes on the other, or similar constructions, are a useful feature.

The camera holder on top of the tripod takes two basic forms—pan/tilt or ball and socket. The pan/tilt seems to be in greater favour these days, perhaps because there have been too many unreliable ball-and-socket constructions. The pan/tilt head consists of a platform with a tripod screw to secure the camera. The platform may be hinged at one end to allow the camera to be held upright or horizontally. There must be a positive stop and lock for both positions.

A long, straight handle allows the head to be turned completely through 360° in the horizontal plane or tilted forward or back through more than 90° in each direction. The handle has a twist lock (usually for the pan only). Most models have a separate tilt lock which is ideal for movie work. Single-locking types are quicker for still work. That is the basic pan/tilt head. The points to watch for, apart from ease of operation and positive locks, are the accessibility of the tripod screw (it is sometimes awkwardly placed under the platform) and the size of the platform. A large platform is useful for larger format cameras, but 35 mm cameras are small and any undue front to back length of the platform can foul protruding knobs or levers on some lenses.

A ball-and-socket head is in several parts. A ball with tripod screw attached is passed through a substantial tube with a cupped hole at the top. A camera platform, generally small and circular, is fastened over the protruding tripod screw. The ball can then tilt to a limited extent in all directions, while a cut in the edge of the cup allows it to tilt the tripod screw into a horizontal position at that point only. The ball is pressed upward in the tube by a cylinder with a cupped top and a screw socket in the bottom to attach it to the tripod. A locking screw passing through the side of the tube forces the cylinder upward relative to the tube so that the ball is gripped by the two cup faces and so locked in any required position.

That is the basic ball and socket. It is a simple and versatile assembly that some prefer to the pan/tilt head because of its greater range of movements. Its disadvantage is that each movement disturbs the horizontal alignment of the camera. More important is that the lock is a rather brutal arrangement that can lead to rapid wear if poor quality metal is used.

You can mount a ball and socket on a pan/tilt head to get the best of both worlds but it is a clumsy arrangement. There are commercial models combining the two types, however, and much more sophisticated mountings for effortless movement of the camera in almost any direction. Gearing can be incorporated, for example, with or without levels and scales, to allow minute and measurable alterations in camera position. These more advanced heads are of greater interest to movie camera users, who need the smoothest possible movement, but they have their applications in specialist still camera work.

The sturdiness of a tripod is naturally the most important factor. If it is to be used in a studio, weight need not be too much of a problem and it can even be put on wheels to aid manoeuvrability. But the portable tripod must not be too heavy, so it has to rely on its construction to provide rigidity. Unfortunately, aids to rigidity often militate against versatility.

Bracing the legs together undoubtedly adds strength, but it also prohibits unequal leg angles to cope with difficult ground and the wide spreading of the legs for low level work. The bracing struts can be made telescopic, but that adds to the weight and cost. If the legs can be locked absolutely positively at the top, you may manage without bracing, but that is only an advantage if the legs can be really widely splayed.

Tripod accessories

Apart from the alternative heads that can be attached to tripods (ball-and-socket and pan/tilt are generally interchangeable), there are various accessories connected with their use. Among these, perhaps the most useful is the quick release shoe. Attaching a camera to a tripod can be an awkward business that takes, at best, several seconds and is hard on the fingers. There is a temptation to overtighten the screw which sometimes damages the camera. An easy way out is to attach a shoe to the tripod head and a complementary clip to the camera, bellows, long lens, etc. The shoe stays on the tripod permanently, while the clip can be transferred to the appropriate piece of equipment as required. You can have two or three clips if you like (they are sold separately) and leave them permanently attached to equipment that is always used on a tripod.

There are various commercial designs. In one of the most popular, you simply slide the clip over the shoe until it locks. There is an additional safety lock to prevent accidental operation of the removal lever, which you simply press in to slide the assembly off the shoe. It is virtually an instantaneous operation.

You use a tripod to hold the camera steady so there is little sense in operating the shutter release with your finger in the normal way. A cable release is essential, but not, perhaps, if your camera is fitted with a self-timer, because that is a perfectly satisfactory way of releasing the shutter for static subjects.

The basic design of a cable release is a springy metal cable in a flexible sheath. A rod with button top at one end exerts damped pressure on a rod or pin at the other end. A separate spring returns the push rod, pulling the operating pin with it, as pressure is released. The end of the sheath has a fitting to allow it to screw into or attach to the shutter release button. The standard design is a small tapered thread. Adapters are available to convert the standard design to fit cameras using other designs.

The springiness of the cable is designed to allow it to be operated in a curved position and also to absorb any hand movement so that it is not transmitted to the camera. A cable release should, in fact, always be operated slackly. It should never be pulled taut because that negates its function as a 'shock absorber'.

Cable releases are available in various lengths and qualities. The popular type is relatively flimsy with a thin woven cover. Stronger types with heavier plastic covering and strong metal fitments are

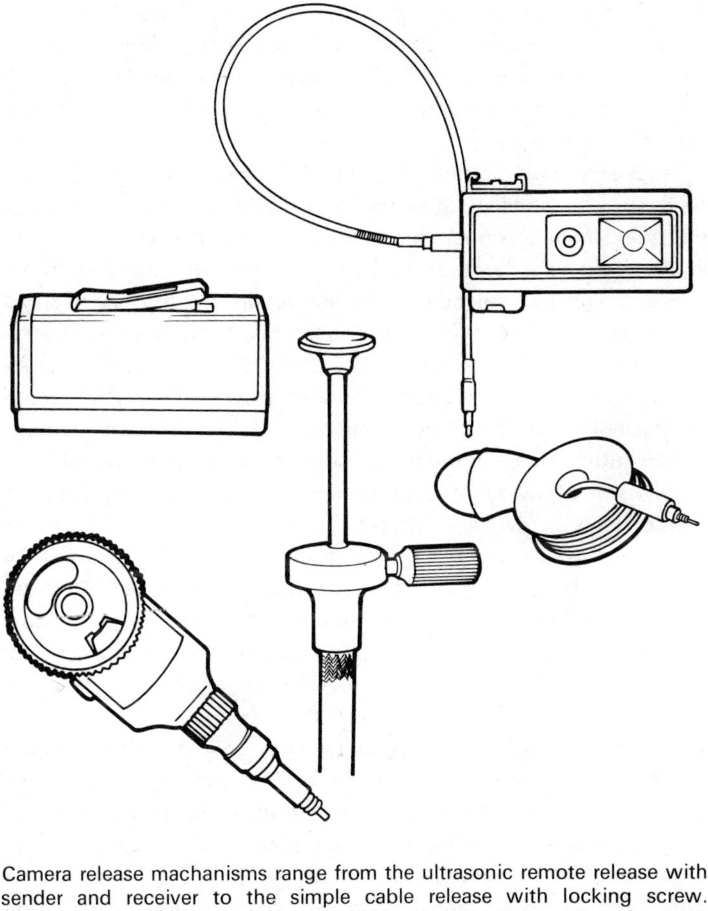

Camera release machanisms range from the ultrasonic remote release with sender and receiver to the simple cable release with locking screw. 'Remote' control can also be achieved by long air release with rubber bulb or by a self-timer. For cameras without a self-timer, an accessory can be screwed into the camera release.

worth looking for if you want a release longer than about 15 cm. Locking types are also available, allowing you to lock the shutter open for long time exposures. The lock may be a disc around the plunger operating on a push and twist principle or a simple pinch screw. The screw is generally safer. The disc type tends to be easily unlocked by accident.

An alternative to a cable release is an air release. The operating pin is moved by air pressure supplied by a small hand bulb. An advantage is that the air tube can be longer than a cable—6 metres or more. It has to be looked after carefully however. The slightest leak makes the release inoperative, and it might be difficult to find the leak in a hurry.

A more expensive method of operation is by ultrasonic radiation. A two-part unit consists of sender and receiver. The receiver plugs into the camera's shutter release socket, either directly or connecting to it via a cable. It works from a dry cell, the signal from the sender operating a solenoid in the receiver up to a distance of about 12 metres. The delay is about 0.2 second and current consumption is relatively high at 400 mA. Unlike radio-wave-operated controls, the ultrasonic unit does not need a licence in the United Kingdom.

Increasingly more cameras are being equipped with electromagnetic shutter release buttons. These models can often be released by any sort of switch, and so a range of remote radio or infra-red controllers and interval timers are available.

The self-timer or delayed action shutter release can be used for shake-free shooting but not all cameras are so equipped. Provided there is a cable release socket, that need not be an insuperable problem. You can buy a small spring-operated timer to screw into the socket. A popular model gives variable delays up to 20 seconds.

A tripod bar can be useful for cameras that have their tripod sockets at one end of the camera. That can lead to a very unbalanced tripod. The bar has a screw fitting for the camera bush and provides a further bush or socket nearer the camera centre. This type of attachment has been made for specific cameras and, in some cases, more elaborate camera cradles have been made available for the same purpose.

If you want to put a flash unit on a tripod, a useful little gadget is

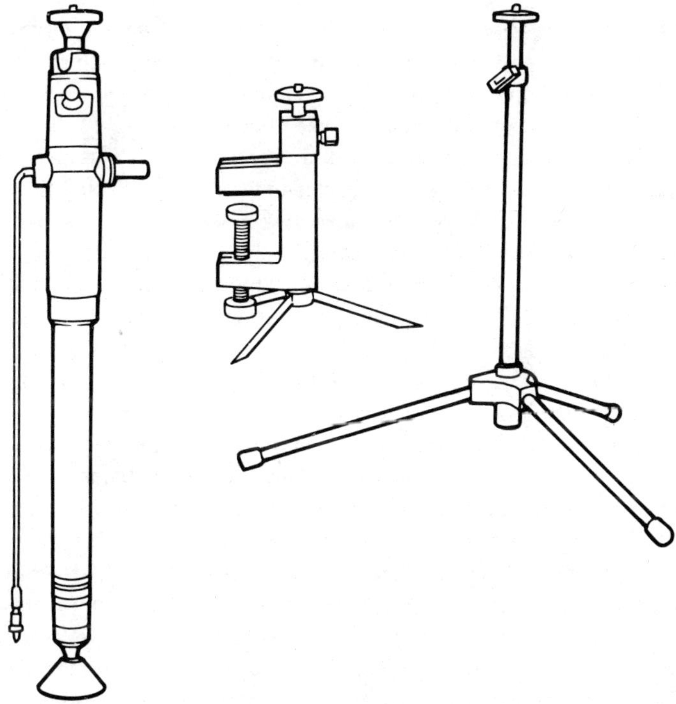

More easily portable alternatives to the tripod are a monopod (*left*), camera clamp (*centre*) or mini-tripod. Each is available in simple or relatively sophisitcated form.

an accessory shoe fastened to a tripod bush. Simply screw the unit on to your tripod head and the flash unit slips into the shoe.
There is even a tripod hanger that screws on to the tripod screw and provides a ring to enable you to hang the tripod on a convenient hook.
A poor relation of cable and air releases is the soft-touch button. It screws into the shutter release button and provides a larger and sometimes pressure-absorbent surface. It can help with cameras that have rather inaccessible release buttons and is particularly useful for the gloved or over-large-fingered cameraman.

Other camera supports

A tripod is the most versatile, but not the only, camera support. There are others, varying from the humble bean bag to the sophisticated copy stand. Copy stands and other close-up equipment are dealt with in a separate chapter.
The bean bag has been around for a very long time. Whether you buy one or make your own rather depends on your DIY ability and how much you care about the looks of your equipment. The idea is to provide a floppy but reasonably firm bag that can mould itself into various shapes to fit over a car window frame, chair back, wall, tree branch, etc. Then you push your camera or long lens into its yielding surface and have surprisingly firm support. It does not lend itself easily to precise framing but is perfectly serviceable and far better than an unsupported shot.
You can buy the bag ready filled or empty. The filling can be dried peas, lentils, plastic granules or any similar substance. The commercial product is made from tough fabric with a zip closure, so that it can be emptied, washed and refilled.
A step up the scale is a camera clamp. The popular variety is similar to the woodworkers G-cramp but has a small ball and socket head and, usually, a detachable spike or screw to enable it to be fixed to a fence post, tree trunk, etc. Screw-in legs are sometimes supplied to convert the clamp to a mini-tripod for very small cameras. Others tend to overbalance it all too easily.
True mini-tripods come in various forms. We refer here to genuinely small tripods extending to a maximum of about 30 cm

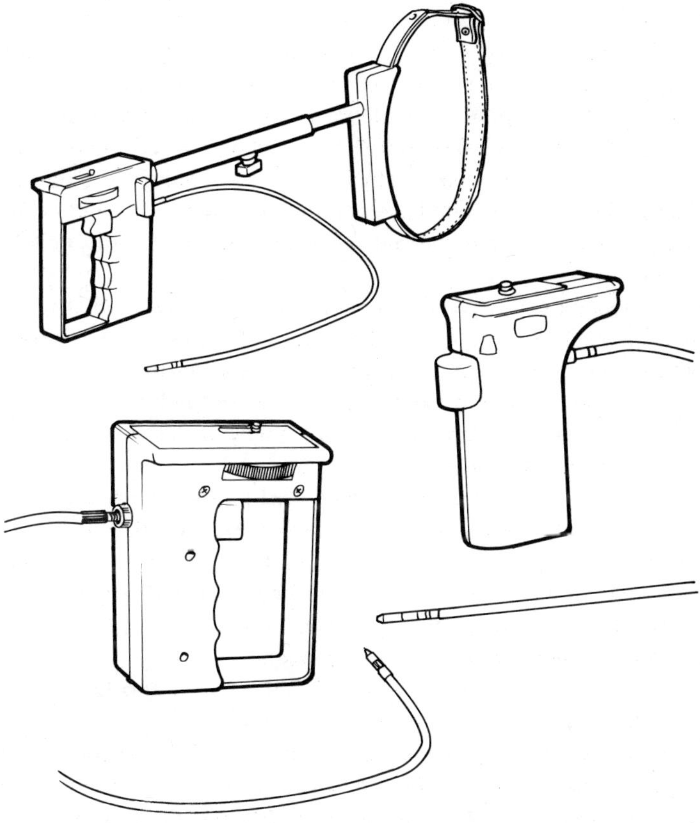

When a tripod cannot be used, aids to a steady camera hold include the rifle grip and pistol grip, each available in many forms. Both types generally incorporate trigger operation linked to a cable release.

and designed for the purpose. There are many of the full-sized variety that collapse to a small size, but in their case collapse is often the operative word.

The mini or table tripod is designed to be carried everywhere and to be used on walls, car roofs and other supports taking the place of the normal tripod elevation. They are often so designed that they can be used, with their legs folded in, as hand grips or as chestpods, with the legs pressing against the chest and the camera tilted on the ball and socket to level it.

Full-size tripods are a little clumsy in use. The three legs are not easy to manage and one always seems to trap the unwary foot. There is such a thing, however, as a unipod, or monopod, with only one leg topped by a tripod screw. Elaborate versions are produced with ball-and-socket head, cable release and other excesses, but all that seems rather to defeat the object. The unipod is a simple, easily-operated camera support that can be tilted in any direction. If you need the full range of movements, you need a tripod.

If you really need a camera support (as you do with most long-focus lenses) but find it too clumsy for your type of work—sport, perhaps, or birds in flight, involving your continual movement from point to point—a rifle grip may solve your problems. A well-designed rifle grip can give a surprisingly steady hold and is relatively easy to carry in ready-to-shoot form.

Designs vary. A simple, popular type consists of a sturdy rod, with shaped shoulder rest and strap at one end and a pistol type butt at the other with trigger-operated cable release. A camera or long-lens platform with tripod screw is attached to the rod. The platform is adjustable for position on the rod and the rod itself can be extended to allow for arm-length variations.

More sophisticated designs support both camera and lens barrel and are often tailored to specific cameras and lenses.

Pistol grips also follow the gun analogy but are not nearly so steady in use. They are designed more or less like the butt of a pistol but with tripod screw or quick attachment on top and a trigger- or button-operated cable release. Their applications are limited but some photographers find them easy to use when resting a long lens on a bean bag, wall, fence, etc. or in the crook of the arm. They demand such two-point support, being rather ineffective used in any other way. They are more likely to cause camera shake than prevent it.

Cases and Containers

As you collect extra bits of camera equipment—lenses, filters, flashguns, etc.—the problem of how to carry them about arises. There are various solutions.

Camera cases

Most cameras are supplied in or with a so-called ever-ready case. This name goes back a long way but today the name is rarely applicable. In its many forms, the ever-ready case has one feature that is common to all. The part that covers the lens is hinged or press-studded or eyeletted in such a way that it can be dropped down to hang below the camera or, in some, removed altogether. Just a quick flip and the camera is fully operational.

That was the original idea. It was never very successful even before 35 mm cameras became bumpy and often bulky objects. Now that so many photographers habitually carry around a camera with considerable lumps of glass and metal on the front, 'ever-ready' is a very misleading description. The front flap is substantial, often unyielding and a real nuisance, particularly when the camera is turned for vertical-format pictures. You may be able to remove that part of the case, but the best solution is probably to leave it at home.

Perhaps half an ever-ready case is better than none. At least it protects the body from knocks that might spoil its professional black paint. To set off against that doubtful advantage, it is clumsy, invariably badly designed and hinders rather than helps rapid operation. It is odd, too, that so many manufacturers, after making a sales point of the material covering the camera body, and even the shape of the body, then put it in a smooth plastic case of indeterminate shape that is difficult to grip.

As camera design becomes more complicated, the case has to be pierced with holes to allow the fingers to get at the controls. It has to be cut down to allow those sophisticated edge controls to be used. It must be taken off, of course, to attach a power winder or, usually, a flash bracket. In other words, it is a useless dust trap.

It is generally wisest to put the case away carefully when you first buy the camera and preserve it against the time when you want to sell the camera or trade it in. It might add a little to the used value of the camera.

Cases for lenses

Most lenses are supplied in tubular cases with flip tops. Some have one flat side so that they don't roll about. Quality varies, of course, but many of them are little better than paper-covered cardboard boxes lined with dust-collecting pseudo felt.

If you carry your camera about with just one extra lens and no other equipment, the lens case on a strap could be useful. In that event, check your case carefully and consider buying a better one if it looks flimsy. If you carry various pieces of equipment in a holdall or gadget bag, the lens case is superfluous. It adds weight, increases the size of the holdall you have to carry and offers little extra protection. It also makes lens changing a considerable chore. There is not much point in having the cleanest lenses possible if you never manage to fit them on the camera in time to take the picture.

The habit of using a lens case and dispensing with front and rear caps is indefensible. A case inevitably accumulates a lot of dust and debris and, in its confines all that finds its way on to and into the lens. If added protection is needed inside your holdall, a plastic bag, frequently renewed, is a better choice. But always keep the caps on.

Soft cases and pouches

Some manufacturers offer soft ever-ready cases that are a lot easier to use than the hard variety, but they still have that often massive, always tiresome, front flap. For smaller cameras, however, there are soft pouches that are very serviceable. These cameras, such as modern compacts and the half-frames that have now almost disappeared, are often much more conveniently carried in a soft pouch on a wrist strap. The pouch is quickly zipped apart and then falls right off the camera and hangs on the strap. Alternatively, a soft pouch is usually flexible enough to be stuffed in the pocket.

Soft pouches or bags that can be completely closed, sometimes on a drawstring are very useful for lenses. They are longer lasting and more efficient than plastic bags and not so dust-attracting as the conventional case.

Holdalls and gadget bags

Once you accumulate more than a camera body and two lenses—and feel the need to carry it all with you—some sort of container becomes obligatory. The options are many.

For several years, a gadget bag was more or less standard in design and many of the traditional type are still in use. This is a box-like case with shoulder strap, generally compartmented inside and with external pockets for small items. The top is zipped or press-studded into place and opens up to allow easy access to the interior with the bag on the shoulder. Later, more ambitious designs, resemble toolboxes with innumerable movable compartment divisions, drop-down sides and even lift-out trays. They remind you of the chest-type deep freezer and some of them are large enough to make the analogy particularly apposite. You sometimes have to unload everything to recover the small item that has found its way to the bottom.

A small well-designed gadget bag can be useful if you discipline yourself to carry just a few essential items. It should be reasonably versatile, however, so that you can vary your equipment for the job in hand. That could mean that you are better off without internal compartments. One day you might want to carry the camera body and two lenses, plus an exposure meter and a filter or two. Another day, you might need extension tubes, a tele-extender and a flashgun.

Cases with variable compartments and external pockets of reasonable capacity are the most versatile. External straps capable of holding a tripod or long lens could be an advantage, although such items are generally more conveniently carried on a shoulder strap.

One problem with a gadget bag, particularly the plushy expensive looking type, is that it advertises its contents. It is obviously a photographic item and could be a temptation for thieves. It can also become very heavy, even with only a few items packed into it. It is not easy to carry on the shoulder, which tends to sag a little and obliges you to ease the weight frequently. With all these problems it is time to think of something else.

If you are excessively thief-conscious and not concerned with self-advertisement, you can use an old holdall or shopping bag that nobody would think contained anything of value. But then the difficulty is that all your equipment needs added protection against bumping around inside the bag. There are innumerable grips and bags on the market now, designed for various purposes and it is worth searching about in travel goods departments for something that can be adapted to your purpose. Strong canvas bags are available in many sizes, often compartmented and with outside pockets. Among the grips offered on the photographic market, there is one with a built-in changing bag. In sports goods stores you might find the shaped, air-cushioned, waterproof bag that floats.

Grips are practicable only for a relatively limited amount of equipment. If you habitually carry a wide range of items with you, the grip becomes difficult to manage and to stow safely. You must think of something much more robust because you are then more concerned with protection than portability. The metal case must then commend itself. There are many types but they are all designed on the one basic principle. The variations are in size, and durability.

The basic design is that of a rigid attaché-type case; a rectangular box with a relatively shallow hinged lid with strong hinges and locks. Most are made from lightweight metal with reinforced edges and corners. The best are strong enough to survive underneath a pile of luggage. The worst give way visibly under finger pressure.

Almost always the inside is filled with a plastic foam block, either custom-made with cut-out shapes for particular outfits or, more usually, for you to cut as required. Spare blocks of foam are readily

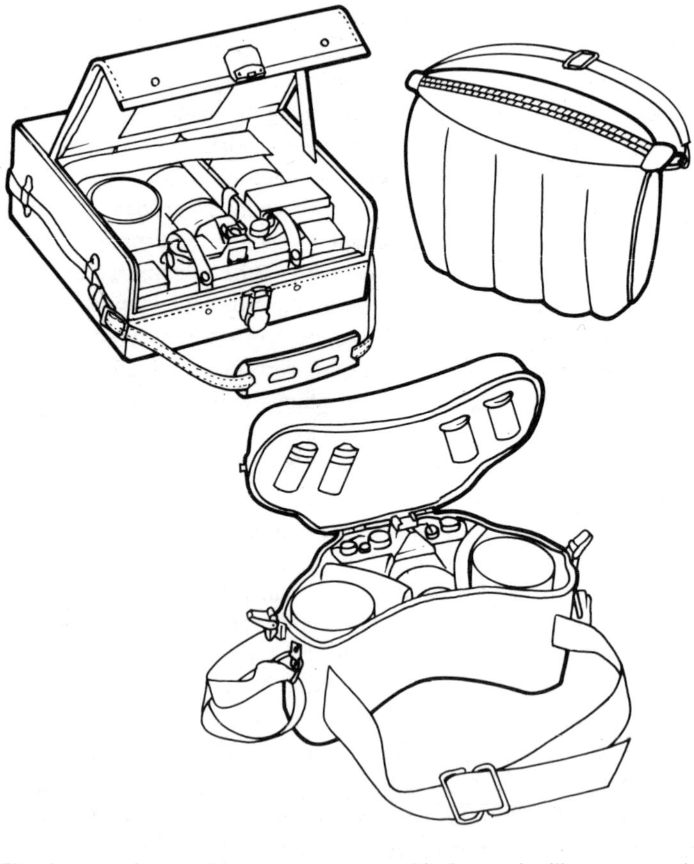

Fitted cases of many designs are popular with those who like to carry a lot of equipment. The shaped case is designed to be strapped around the waist. The pouch is inflatable and provides cushioning against knocks. It also floats.

available. The lid is similarly filled with foam plastic for protection.
Generally, these so-called custom cases are made for transportability rather than portability. As with so many items, however, they became fashionable rather than utilitarian and smaller versions were made to be toted on the shoulder like a gadget bag. They are not ideal for the purpose, being necessarily rigid and not a good shape for this method of carrying. They can bump about painfully on the hip and are, in fact, better carried in the hand.

Each type, the holdall and the custom case, has its followers and there is no point in arguing the merits and demerits. It is a matter of personal choice. Some like the convenience of easily extracting items from a bag sitting more or less on the hip. Others are happy to place a custom case on the ground and open the lid to take the required item from its shaped receptacle.

The larger type of custom case, however, has no equal if you have to carry a lot of equipment. You need a rigid container because the weight of the equipment inside it can be considerable. Most other types of container would tend to pull the items together as they were lifted and carried. The custom case keeps each object virtually immovable but still shock-protected in its foam bed. It is not intended to be carried very far. It is loaded into the transport and possibly spends most of its time there. If you shoot everything from the car door you have no problem, but if you venture far afield another, smaller holdall would be a wise investment. You can carry just the items you need for that exercise, leaving the rest securely locked up in the car.

Cases for small items

Almost everything photographic is either supplied in some sort of case, or a case can be bought for it. About the only exception is a flashgun which is apparently not thought to need added protection.

For the travelling-light brigade, there is even a small case to fit on your carrying strap, designed to carry just one film in its carton. That could make sense on some trips when you have a clear idea of how many shots you are going to take.

If you expect to use more than one film, you can take along the

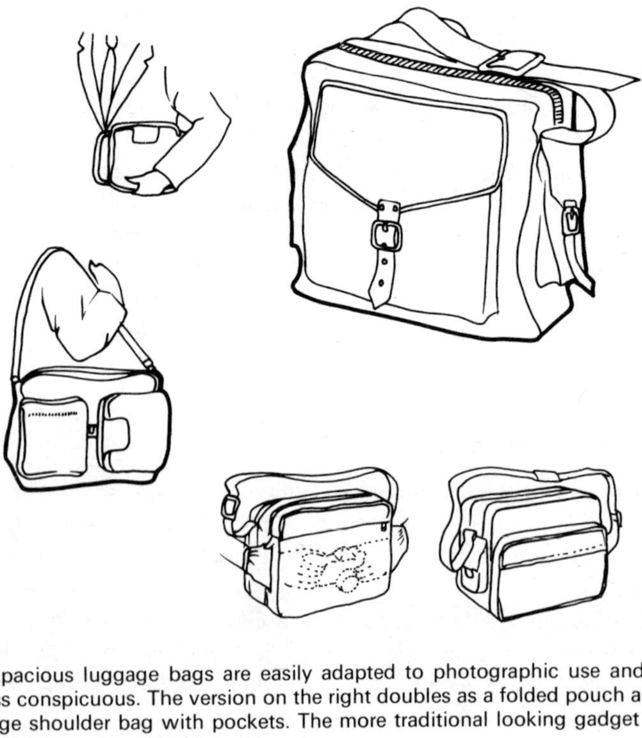

Capacious luggage bags are easily adapted to photographic use and are less conspicuous. The version on the right doubles as a folded pouch and a large shoulder bag with pockets. The more traditional looking gadget bag has its own changing bag.

jumbo version in the form of a film dispenser that holds up to four 35 mm films in cassettes. It clips on to a belt or camera strap. Incidentally, the box in which most processors return your slides takes four 35 mm cassettes snugly. The transparent ones even let you see what is inside.

Now that battery-powered shutters are commonly used, it is a wise precaution always to carry a spare battery. Many camera manufacturers are now including small, strap-attaching cases for that very purpose in their lists of accessories.

Filters are rather vulnerable in a gadget bag. If yours does not afford them adequate protection, there are two alternatives. You can buy a filter purse in the form of a flat, zipped wallet with padded pockets. A popular model has pockets made from transparent plastic sheet on a white padded base. It takes up to four filters and you can easily identify their colour through the pockets.

Alternatively you can screw all your filters together and put caps on back and front to make a sealed stack. It may may be less convenient but it offers first-class protection.

Choosing and using cases

You don't often get a choice of case. When you buy your equipment the case comes with it, sometimes at an incredible extra cost. It does not seem to be such common practice now but in the early days of price-cutting, some dealers tried to compete by advertising very low prices for the equipment and putting an astronomical cost on the obligatory case. It still happens occasionally, so watch out for it.

Sometimes a camera manufacturer offers a choice of soft or hard case. Generally, the soft case is the better choice. Hard cases are very unwieldy, particularly when they allow for bulky lenses. Of course, they look more impressive, especially when trimmed with metal edges and stuck-on badges, but they are not very practical.

Few cases are now made from leather. There was a time when the stiffness of your new case did not matter as it would soon wear in and become reasonably soft and pliable. When the modern hard case becomes soft and pliable, it generally means that the

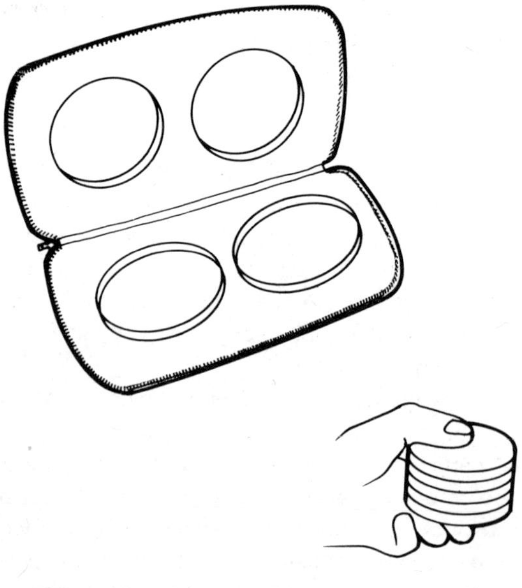

Filters are easily damaged but total protection is afforded by padded cases tailored to filter sizes. Alternatively, the filters can be screwed together and protected by caps at each end.

cardboard interior has broken up. The paper-like covering on the outside soon follows.

You must consider carefully whether you want to use cases for camera and lenses. Once you put the camera in a case, you tend to become careless in handling it. You *think* it is fully protected, but the only real protection you have is against casual knocks and bumps. Some cases are so badly designed that they scratch the equipment every time they are opened. Never put a camera in an ever-ready case without a cap over the lens. That press stud on the back of the lid could have been specifically designed to whip back on to the lens as you unfasten it and drop the lid down.

Modern cases are not very fond of moisture, either. If you use an uncased camera in the wet, you wipe it afterwards. If you use it in a case, you tend not to, but the inside of the case is almost certainly wet and may well begin to rot. It certainly does not offer the ideal protection for the camera once damp sets in.

Much the same kind of argument applies to lens cases. They are a useful storage container if you do not intend to use the lens for some time. Then you can cap back and front and store the lens away in its case. Even then, however, you should first put it in a plastic bag. But then there is little need for the case, which offers virtually no protection against either damp or dust.

It is virtually impossible to keep your equipment in shining, as-new condition. If you want to keep it in a reasonable state but have it always ready for use, just take care of it. Carry the camera on a short strap, preferably across the body, rather than slung over one shoulder. Use back and front caps on lenses and a body cap on the camera if you put it away with no lens attached. Place the equipment carefully into your holdall; do not drop it in. Plastic bags or soft pouches can give added protection if you feel it necessary.

When choosing a holdall or case, think carefully about your requirements. A large case soon becomes a problem as it tempts you to pack in everything you own, and then add something more to prevent the equipment rattling about. You then find you can barely lift it, let alone carry it around.

If you really have to carry a lot of equipment—and that can only be when you are travelling and might take a variety of different types of shots—you probably need a rigid custom case. But it should be your base camp and should be supplemented by another, smaller holdall to take on actual shooting trips. Unless, again, you never have to stray from your transport. That can happen on some occasions—but it is doubtful if you would need all that equipment in the first place.

Custom cases are expensive, so it is best to examine them before you buy. Pay particular attention to locks, hinges and corners, especially if the case may have to travel as luggage. It is not a good idea to buy a small custom case with the intention of carrying it over any distance. It either puts one hand out of action or, if carried on the shoulder, can be awkward, or even painful.

Choosing and Handling Films

The variety of films available can be quite confusing, especially for the users of the 35 mm format and larger. Cartridge-loaded films in the 126 and 110 sizes are more difficult to find. There is only one black-and-white film generally available, and that of medium speed.

These cameras are really intended for colour print work, and there the later 110 versions are reasonably well catered for by the leading manufacturers and various chain stores. Films of 80–100 and 400ASA are readily available.

The ASA figure is a direct indication of comparative fim sensitivity. The 400ASA film is four times as sensitive to light as the 100ASA film and can therefore be used at much lower light levels or at greater distances with a given flash unit.

Those using 126 film have to be satisfied with 100ASA film as their fastest colour negative or colour print version. There is a reasonable choice among the leading makers.

Neither type of camera is particularly well suited to colour slide production and that is reflected in the availability of only one, rather slow (64ASA), film being generally available.

Black-and-white films

All major manufacturers produce a wide range of black-and-white films but not all sell internationally. For many years, the standard general purpose film has been the 125ASA version typified by Kodak Plus-X and Ilford FP4. It gives good contrast, virtually grain-free results at any reasonable degree of enlargement and plenty of tolerance toward less than ideal exposure. As emulsion chemistry improves, however, the faster Tri-X and HP5, at 400ASA, are becoming more popular. They give better contrast and finer grain than was previously expected of fast film and have wide tolerance. Above all, they can be push-processed quite satisfactorily to give the effect of greater film speed in suitable conditions. It is the effectiveness of push-processing, in fact, that has eclipsed the few films faster than 400ASA, that have been produced at various times. Those that remain are generally used only in really extreme conditions.

Slower films are still produced, such as Kodak Panatomic-X at 32ASA, Ilford Pan F at 50ASA, and the revived Adox in some markets, at 20 and 40ASA. Slow films are useful when you are striving for the utmost in fine detail at great enlargements or when shooting at large apertures in bright light. Their exposure tolerance is not great, however, and they have to be handled very carefully. Their extra-fine-grain capability is destroyed by the slightest overexposure or overdevelopment.

There are many special types of black-and-white film. Agfa-Gevaert, for instance, have a 35 mm reversal or slide film that gives black-and-white slides directly in the camera or by copying positive images. So-called positive film, on the other hand, is not designed for camera use. With a very slow emulsion (about 6–10ASA) similar to that used on bromide paper, it is primarily intended to be printed on from a negative. Various versions are available with panchromatic or orthochromatic sensitization.

Other print films are generally provided in the form of sheets. 'Line' and 'lith' are common designations. Both are high contrast films, again with varying types of sensitization, and are designed to produce solid black and clear film images. They are particularly suitable for copying line illustrations and, for the greatest contrast, are processed in special developers. They are used in many 'derivation' techniques, such as solarization and posterization. Processed in bromide paper developers, they can give a reasonable half-tone image at a single step, or a 'line' image with repeated reprintings through positive and negative.

There is also an infra-red sensitive film, usable with various densities of red filter on light source or camera lens, to record images by red light or infra-red radiation only. Such a fiim can be useful for shooting in unlighted areas without attracting too much attention, or for images of striking contrast of landscape, architecture, etc.

Choosing black-and-white film

The type of film you choose depends entirely on the type of work you do—and your personal preference for a particular type of image. Each manufacturer's film has slightly different characteristics that may appeal to one photographer and not to another. There is no best film and no bad film among the well-known brands.

It is pointless to be influenced by another person's choice unless he happens to do exactly the same sort of work as you. Press photographers are likely to favour 400ASA film for most of their work because it can be used in almost any lighting conditions. Professional photographers in general may use almost any film. Like amateurs, they often have a variety of interests. Those primarily engaged in studio work on still life objects may use flash a lot and therefore could choose a slow film. Medium speed film is likely to be the choice of those doing a variety of work but rarely shooting fast-moving subjects at low light levels. Which brand they use can depend on a variety of things, most of which are personal to the user.

Your choice should be similarly decided. A few years ago the advice would unhesitatingly have been that you should choose a 125ASA film because it can cope with almost any subject you are likely to attempt. Faster films were purely for low light levels and gave rather inferior results. This is no longer the case, so you can consider a 400ASA film as your first choice if you like to have that little extra sensitivity in hand.

You must remember, however, that a 400ASA film is rather over-sensitive for sunny lighting conditions. It might need an exposure in the region of 1/500 second at *f*16 or *f*11, leaving *f*8 as the maximum aperture you could use on most cameras. That could give you a lot more depth of field than you want. There are ways round the problem. You can use coloured or neutral density filters or you can adjust your processing. If you find yourself doing that very often, you are using the wrong film.

Colour print films

Films designed for the production of colour prints are commonly called colour print film or colour negative film—the latter because

they produce a negative image from which prints can be made.
There is a reasonable choice of colour negative film in most markets, again with varying sensitivity. Generally, the choice is between 80, 100 and 400ASA. Most people looking for quality images may still tend to go for the 80 or 100ASA versions. Fast films are relatively new in the field and are no doubt still developing. At present the quality of the image they produce is good but they might have been improved still further before release but for the advent of 110 cameras. The popular versions of these cameras are somewhat limited in their applications with 100ASA film. The faster film gives them much greater versatility.
As with black-and-white film, personal preference plays a large part in the choice of colour print film. Your type of work does not have so much influence because the 400ASA film is definitely for those who do a lot of low-light work, dull weather shooting, etc. It seems to revel in those conditions but has not a lot to commend it for general work.
Personal preference, on the other hand, plays a greater part than with black-and-white film because colour rendering is inevitably slightly different with each brand.

Colour slide film

Films designed for the production of colour slides are commonly called colour reversal or colour slide film—the latter because they produce positive colour images directly on the film used in the camera. The colour reversal name comes from the type of processing. The original image produced on the film is negative in the normal way but it is reversed to a positive by a slightly more complicated processing method.
The choice is a little wider than with colour negative film because there are two types—daylight and artificial light. Colour negative film can be used in either type of lighting, because it is subsequently used to produce prints. Filters can be used to adjust the colour of the printing light. That is not possible with a colour slide, which is produced as the film is processed. So different versions are supplied to allow for the difference in colour quality between daylight (bluish) and artificial light (yellowish).

There are fewer artificial light films than there used to be. At one time, all major manufacturers offered a film designed for the amateur's most popular form of lighting—at that time the overrun photoflood of 3400 K. With the turnover to flash and most of the demand for artificial light film coming from professionals, the emphasis shifted to films for studio type lighting at 3200 K. These are photopearls, the more powerful studio-type tungsten lamps and most photographic tungsten-halogen lamps.

The biggest choice is in daylight films. Ideally, they are intended for use in good sunlight with a reasonable amount of light cloud to reflect the light and subdue excess blue from the sky itself. Such light has a colour temperature of about 5500–6000 K. Electronic flashguns are made to produce a light of similar quality and daylight film can therefore be used with electronic flash, too. It can be used with flashbulbs provided they have a blue coating, as most of the smaller types do.

The range of sensitivities in daylight films is generally from 25, to 400ASA with 50, 64, 100 and 200 popular choices in between. Again, the choice depends largely on personal preference. Kodak's 25ASA Kodachrome has probably survived because of the popularity of the type of image it produces—virtually grainless and capable of extreme enlargement to show the finest detail. It also has a warm colour rendering that its adherents find pleasing. Naturally, not everybody agrees with them, some people preferring what they consider the more natural rendering of the so-called professional films.

Special colour films

Apart from the colour print and colour slide films designed for ordinary camera use, there are two main specialist films.

Kodak's Infra-red Aero Ektachrome was, as its name implies, developed for aerial survey work of a specialized kind. It has been taken up by some general photographers because of the extraordinary effects it can provide. It is deliberately designed to produce false colours, such as magenta foliage and, in the right hands, it can be used to good creative effect—but not too often.

Slide duplicating film is rather more mundane. Colour slide film generally gives strong contrasts and is difficult to copy on to another, equally contrasty film. Slide duplicating film has a softer contrast characteristic designed specifically for the task. It is generally supplied only in bulk lengths of 30 m or 100 ft.

How to buy your film

You do not have a lot of choice in the packings of colour film you can buy. Naturally, cartridge-camera users buy theirs in the cartridge, perhaps with a choice of 12 or 20 exposures in colour negative.

Roll and sheet film users are similarly circumscribed. Users of 35 mm film, however, have the option of 12-, 20-, 24- or 36-exposure/loaded cassettes in both colour negative and colour slide film and one or two brands in lengths of 5, 10, 15 and 30 m for loading into their own cassettes.

Bulk supplies are much more common in black-and-white (35 mm only), most brands being available in lengths of 5, 17 and 30 m.

Where you buy your film is important. Black-and-white films have a long life (several years) and you are unlikely to run into trouble with any normal film outlet. Nevertheless, if possible, it is just as well to buy from a supplier you know has a reasonable turnover of stock—and that is not always a photographic dealer.

Much more care is needed with colour film. Ideally, it should be refrigerated but most films survive with ordinary cool storage for a reasonable period. If you see a stack of films in a flimsy rack over a radiator or in direct sunlight, avoid that dealer. Look at the expiry date on the packet. If it is around six months or less ahead, that shop has a poor turnover and you would be wise to find another supplier.

When you have bought your colour film, store it sensibly or, preferably, use it and get it processed quickly. Sensible storage does not always mean refrigeration. That calls for a few hours thawing out before you open the packet and could do more harm than good. Store the film in the coolest, driest place you can find.

Film accessories

There are various accessories connected with the handling of film, the most obvious being spare cassettes and a loader for those who decide to buy their film in bulk lengths.

You can re-use the cassettes you buy full of film, or you can buy other people's used cassettes or new, usually plastic, reloadable cassettes. You can even buy the fixing tape to attach the end of the film to the cassette spool. Designed for the job, it does not ooze adhesive and is a better proposition than ordinary adhesive tape. Masking tape is generally satisfactory.

You can load cassettes by hand with practice but you would be well advised to buy a bulk film loader. There are several types of similar design. The basic arrangement is a light-tight chamber to hold up to 30 m or 100 ft of film. It has a slot leading to the cassette chamber that is opened only when the cassette chamber is closed. In the cassette chamber is a drive mechanism connected to an external handle and a frame counter. Once the film chamber is loaded you can operate in daylight to load cassettes with any length of film up to 36 frames.

Having loaded your cassette, you can even buy reload labels to stick on them to identify the film. They can then be put in cassette containers to protect them from dust and damp. When you load them into the camera, you can use yet another identifier—a pocket that attaches to the back of the camera and is intended to take the top of a film carton. If you have bulk-loaded, you have to make your own label.

If you find it difficult to dismantle the cassette to attach the film end, that too is catered for. There is a tong-like arrangement designed to lever off the end that generally breaks a fingernail. Don't try it on the crimped-end-types which are virtually unopenable without destruction. You have to handle film very carefully when loading cassettes. If your fingers get on the emulsion side, they can leave indelible marks, especially if they are moist or greasy. That eventuality has been provided for too, with the offer of special film-handling gloves.

Finally, you must put the bulk roll of film into the loader in complete darkness. If you have no darkroom, that is a job for a changing bag. This is a useful piece of equipment at any time. It usually takes the form of a large zipped bag with elasticated holes through which you push your arms to complete a light-tight seal.

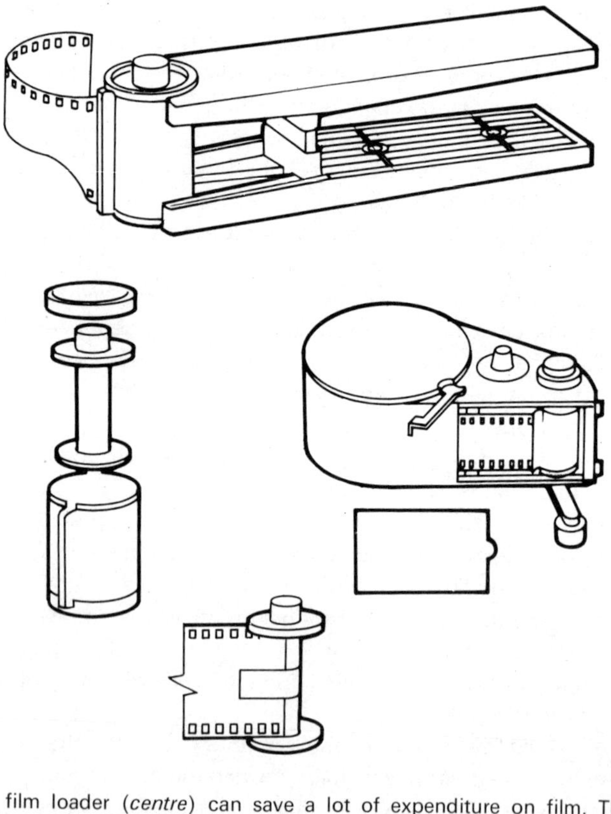

A bulk film loader (*centre*) can save a lot of expenditure on film. The standard cassette (*left*) is easily taken apart for the attachment of the film end to the internal spool. For even easier opening, a special tool is available.

You put all the necessary bits and pieces inside, do up the zip and operate by touch alone, just as if you were in a darkroom but in a rather more confined space.

There is a lot to be said for carrying a changing bag in your case or holdall. Camera troubles are not all that unusual and it is very galling not to be able to open the camera without spoiling the shots you have already taken. There is, as we have already mentioned, a gadget bag that incorporates a changing bag.

Bits and Pieces

There are innumerable odd items available to the photographer that defy classification. They appear in press advertisements, mail order catalogues and shop windows and, in many cases, are designed to catch the passing trade or the impulse buyer. They are often very attractively packed.

We have already dealt with a few of these in the form of adapters, camera clamps, mini tripods, cable releases, etc. while there are others for darkroom and film processing use that are outside the scope of this book. Here, we gather together the few oddments that do not fall naturally into precise chapters.

Carrying straps

Few cameras are easily carried in the hand and the normal mode of transport is to suspend the camera about the person by means of a strap. Ever-ready cases are invariably fitted with straps but not everybody likes these cases, so a strap fixed to the camera itself is necessary.

Most cameras have lugs near the top corners to take strap fixings. Some straps can attach directly to the small holes in these lugs but the majority use triangular or D-shaped rings to which the strap is clipped, or through which it is passed to double back on itself for fastening with an eyelet and stud arrangement.

Almost without exception, the straps supplied with cameras or on ever-ready cases, are no more than 15 mm wide, often only 10 mm or so. This is a villainous construction. It can dig painfully into your neck or shoulder and make even a relatively lightweight camera an intolerable burden after an hour or two. Shoulder pads that slide up and down the strap also tend to do that, and never seem to stay where they are needed to relieve the pressure.

Perhaps the popularity of electric guitars had something to do with it, because there is now available a wide range of camera straps in widths up to 5 cm (2 in). They are generally of woven material with a belt buckle type of adjustment and strong clips to fit D-rings. To the conventional these straps may look a little extreme and reluctance to attach one to a Leica is readily understandable. But they are a lot more sensible than the orthodox strap and for a heavy camera they are virtually essential.

The narrower straps are, of course, quite suitable for smaller items, including some cameras. Some of these might even be carried on a fashionable snake chain if you wish. One exposure meter at least, was supplied with such a fitment, although the traditional long lanyard of the Weston meters is more sensible. You often need to hold the meter at arm's length and it is convenient to have it still attached to you to prevent dropping it.

Carrying straps are important and should be looked after. We all tend to take them for granted until a vital rivet pops or a nick develops into a rupture and the camera falls to the ground. Inspect your straps regularly for signs of wear and replace them if there is the slightest risk of impending failure. And when you do that, look at the range now available—not necessarily just from photographic dealers.

Wrist straps can be useful for some lightweight cameras that do not fit easily into the pocket and yet are too small to justify a full carrying strap. These can be in the form of a loop rotating on a tripod screw attachment. Make sure that the loop strap can rotate quite freely with the screw stationary or you may find yourself carrying just the tripod screw.

Cleaning items

Cameras and lenses attract dust and fingerprints, and this is unavoidable. Manufacturers have not been slow to provide for the camera-proud. If there is a rule about camera and lens cleaning, it should be 'Don't do it'. Cleanliness is advisable, but ill-advised cleaning can do more harm than good.

Optical glass is not as soft as some would have you think. Now that all lenses are coated, their surfaces stand up reasonably well to somewhat careless treatment. Nevertheless, constant polishing of

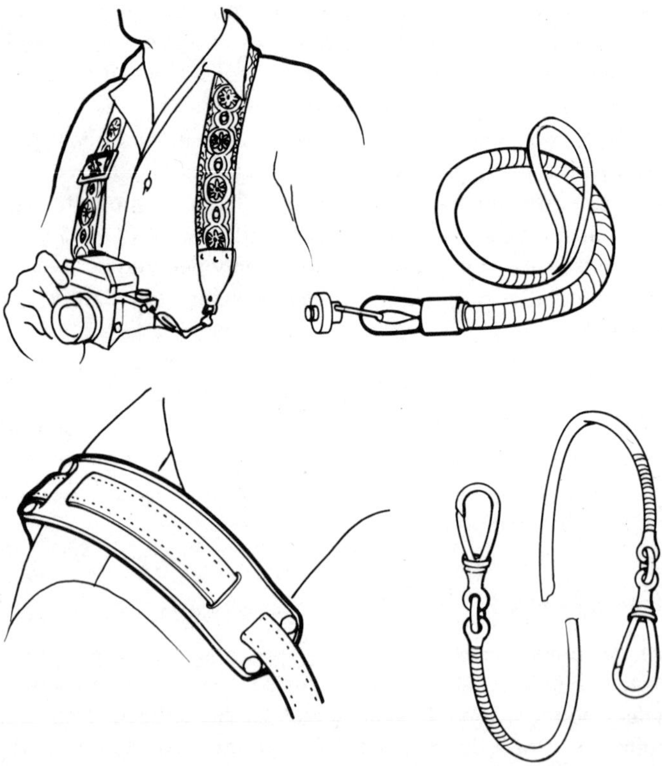

The wide camera strap obviates the need for the shoulder pad so essential with thinner straps. Lightweight cameras can be carried on a wrist strap with tripod screws while even lighter accessories can be attached to an elegant metal neck chain.

the lens surface with a handkerchief or, worse, a lens cleaning tissue, can soon take the edge off its performance, so stick to the gentler methods.

Blower brushes are probably the most useful item. These are soft, stubby brushes on a hollow stem with a small ball attached. Squeezing the ball provides a puff of air to dislodge loose dust. The brush head is generally removable, uncovering a nozzle to concentrate the air jet into corners and crevices. The brush itself should be used gently and only when really necessary to flick dirt out of lens rims, etc.

Photographic lens tissues are made from acid-free material, so that when you rub the tissue all over the lens surface you do not deposit any destructive acid on it. This is a good idea for spectacle wearers, most of whom scrub assiduously at their lenses every day. It is a little pointless for camera users because the tissue should never be used to wipe the lens under finger pressure. It should be folded into a brush shape and used *like* a brush. But in that case, why not use a brush?

The only time you might justify using a lens tissue to wipe your lens is when you have a finger mark on it. That can, indeed, damage the coating and even the glass underneath it. Then you can risk damping the tissue or, preferably, a many-times washed handkerchief, and rubbing the finger mark off as gently as possible.

Never use a polishing cloth at all. You can't keep them clean, no matter how much anti-static treatment they may have. Similarly, there can be hardly any occasion when you need to use lens cleaning fluid, finger marks again being a just possible exception. If your lens is so dirty that you feel a need to give it a bath, it is time it was professionally cleaned.

It does no harm to inspect the inside of your camera now and again and to blow out any dust that might have accumulated. You might even use the brush gently on the mirror and the underside of the screen. Don't touch the mirror with anything else.

Batteries and chargers

Never try to economize on batteries by buying cheaper alternatives. Cameras and flash units are quite expensive and are easily

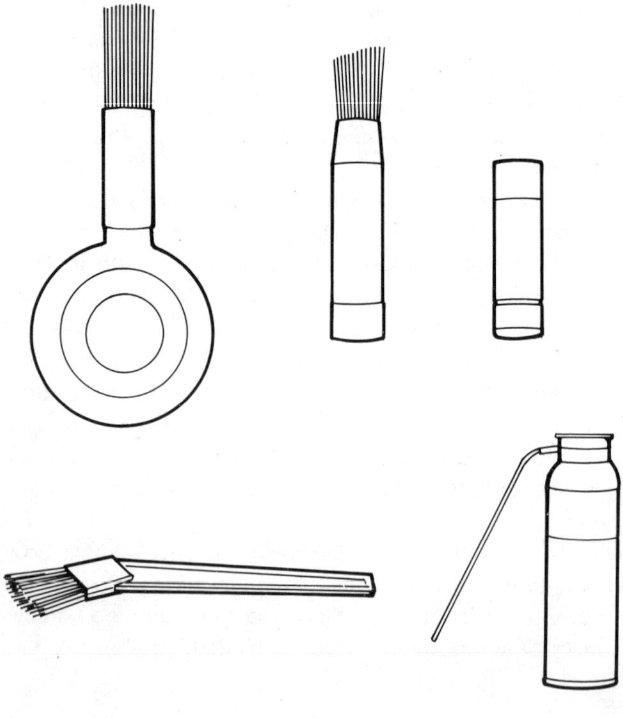

Camera interior and lens brushes can incorporate a blower bulb to help dislodge dust particles, they may be retractable to protect the bristles or they may have angled or swivelling heads. For particularly inaccessible areas, canned compressed air can be useful.

damaged beyond economical repair by leaking batteries. Batteries, generally speaking, are leak-resistant, not leak-proof.

There are several types of battery in regular use in photographic equipment. Those used in cameras for auto-exposure or ordinary TTL meters are generally relatively small button or multiple types of silver or mercury oxide construction. They are expendable and have to be renewed at the end of their life. The camera handbook specifies the type to be used and you should never depart from that. Sometimes only the Japanese reference number is quoted but your dealer can give you the better known Berec, Mallory, Ucar, etc. designation.

In other equipment—flash units, motor drives, etc.—the penlight cell (HP7, Mn1500, etc.) is the most popular. This, like some other dry cells is readily available in the carbon-zinc traditional form or as a manganese alkaline type, both expendable. A rechargeable nickel cadmium type can be used as an alternative.

Carbon-zinc batteries are relatively inexpensive and are generally most suitable for low-current usage. In photographic use, they tend to take high currents so the alkaline types are a better proposition. Their much longer life more than out-weighs the higher cost. Nickel cadmium batteries are much more expensive than even the alkaline types and their life per charge is nearer the carbon-zinc—but you don't throw them away. They can be recharged in about 14 hours at a trickle rate of about 45 mA. Faster charging types are also available.

Battery chargers for nicad batteries are not inexpensive but they do enable you to keep your batteries for a long time and to charge them overnight. The initial outlay can be quite heavy for the charger and, preferably, two sets of batteries.

Choosing batteries

Your choice is generally between nicads and manganese alkaline types—especially for flash use. Carbon-zinc types give only about 50 flashes at best in the average flash gun and even then need rather long recycling times after the first 20 or 30. Their shelf life is not good. Alkaline batteries should give at least four or five times the number of flashes and they can sit unused for very long periods without significant deterioration. The more than occasional user need not worry too much about the condition of his spare set. They will not die while he uses the set in the flash unit.

The same cannot be said for the carbon-zinc type, more likely to be the choice of the occasional user. As they have so short a life in use, and a doubtful shelf life, he should always have a spare set available but preferably should buy them just before the shooting session.

Nickel-cadmium batteries also have the disadvantage of a short life in use plus the necessity for keeping them in good condition. It is not advisable to leave them discharged for long periods. They should, therefore, be the choice only of the regular user who is prepared to carry two sets, with one set constantly on charge.

If you do most of your flash work at home or where mains electricity is available, you can get away with one set by buying the quicker charging type. An hour or so on charge can then put you back in business. In those circumstances, however, you would be better operating with a mains adaptor if possible.

Battery care

All batteries need to be looked after carefully. Camera and flash gun contacts are not very robust and a high resistance to electrical current can be built up by a completely invisible film of corrosion or finger marks. Always, before you decide that batteries are dead—and particularly after a period out of use—remove the batteries and thoroughly clean both battery terminals and the equipment contacts. That will often restore the equipment to full working order.

If you know that you are not going to use the equipment within the next week or two, remove the batteries. Virtually no battery is leakproof and you only have to experience once the havoc a leaking battery can wreak to learn a valuable but costly lesson. Similarly, when you change batteries, *always* change the complete set. Putting a fresh battery in with others that are more or less discharged can burst the case with sufficient force or pressure to break equipment contacts.

Index